WIVES AND SWEETHEARTS

LOVE LETTERS SENT
DURING WARTIME

Alastair Massie
and Frances Parton

NATIONAL
ARMY
MUSEUM

**SIMON &
SCHUSTER**

London · New York · Sydney · Toronto · New Delhi

A CBS COMPANY

First published in Great Britain by Simon & Schuster UK Ltd, 2014
This paperback edition published by Simon & Schuster UK Ltd, 2015
A CBS COMPANY
In association with The National Army Museum

Text copyright © The National Army Museum 2014

1 3 5 7 9 10 8 6 4 2

Simon & Schuster UK Ltd
1st Floor
222 Gray's Inn Road
London WC1X 8HB

www.simonandschuster.co.uk

Simon & Schuster Australia, Sydney
Simon & Schuster India, New Delhi

A CIP catalogue record for this book
is available from the British Library

ISBN: 978-1-47110-265-3
ebook ISBN: 978-1-47112-599-7

The author and publishers have made all reasonable efforts
to contact copyright-holders for permission, and apologise
for any omissions or errors in the form of credits given.
Corrections may be made to future printings.

All photographs are from the archives of the National Army Museum except for
Reginald and Eleanore Stephens on page 31, kindly supplied by Mr Mark Stephens

Typeset by M Rules

Printed and bound by CPI Group (UK) Ltd, Croydon, CR0 4YY

Contents

PART TWO: THE SECOND WORLD WAR
1939–1945

Acknowledgements

For their assistance in the preparation of this book, thanks are due to the following: Colonel Charles Stephens, for permission to quote from the letters of his grandfather, General Sir Reginald Stephens (and Mr Mark Stephens for supplying the splendid photograph of Reginald and his wife, Eleanore); M. Johann Chevillard of the Institut Pasteur, Paris, for clarifying the copyright status of the Duke of Windsor's literary estate; Diana, Lady Farnham; and the National Army Museum interns Barrett Reiter, McLaren Cundiff, Hongjin Du and Katherine Sorresso for their transcribing skills.

At Simon and Schuster we are grateful to Colin Midson for commissioning the book, Kerri Sharp for carrying the project forward, and Sally Partington, our editor, for her sterling work in bringing the volume to press.

Introduction

'Soldiers, like the rest of us, fall in love. Throughout history and according to the conventions of the time, soldiers have flirted with, dated, or courted a partner. In some ways, it can be much easier to meet a sweetheart as a soldier than a civilian; soldiers travel across the globe and meet all sorts of people. In other ways, being a soldier can make meeting and settling down with someone much harder. In addition, a relationship with a serving soldier naturally brings concern for their safety. Despite the difficulties, however, relationships flourish. Some remain casual, but others ultimately lead to an engagement, marriage and a life together.'

This encapsulation of the soldier's romantic experience appeared on the first panel of the National Army Museum's exhibition *Wives and Sweethearts: Love on the Front Line,* which opened on 14 February 2011 in the presence of Dame Vera Lynn, the Forces' sweetheart *par excellence.* Gratifyingly, the exhibition proved a great success, and it therefore seemed a natural next step to create a permanent record of some of its content, this book being the result.

All the stories chosen for inclusion are drawn exclusively from letters and diaries held within the National Army Museum's archives. Where stories are carried over from the exhibition they have been considerably amplified, allowing the trajectory of an attachment to become more readily apparent. Other stories, entirely new to the public, have been extracted from the archives and added to the book afresh. This broader sweep means that one can now read about the romantic tribulations of both the highest in the land and the lowest, from Edward Prince of Wales to the humblest private soldier.

Given that much of the book relates to the First World War, it is appropriate it should be published in 2014, the centenary of the war's outbreak. While much ink will no doubt be expended analysing the wider historical significance of the conflict, it is often good at such a time to step back and consider the human dimension to great events; not in terms of the suffering inseparable from strife but from the more uplifting perspective of love and romance. Even in wartime, aspects of normal life had to continue, and nothing is more normal than for a man and a woman – or, in this case, a soldier and a woman – to fall in love, continue in love, or maybe simply to seize the moment.

The letters that feature in this book have been selected to represent as broad a cross-section as possible of the British soldier's interaction with the women in his life. All the major theatres of war are covered and each individual story placed in a chronological framework, enabling the reader to gauge how the character of relationships changes as the First and Second World Wars progress. For example, it is altogether redolent of a vanished age to realize how the marital status of the full-time regular soldier of 1914 was governed, for officers at least, by the old army adage that 'subalterns may not marry, captains might marry, majors should marry, and lieutenant-colonels must marry'. As a consequence, marriage was delayed until promotion had been achieved, and the senior officers who feature in the early part of the book tended to possess much younger wives. For the latter, as we will see, an army marriage often took on the quality of a condominium: they maintained a keen interest in their husband's career, fulfilled a role within the regiment looking after the welfare of soldiers' wives, were a sounding board for professional grievances and provided a valued support in times of acute stress.

For other-rank soldiers, before the First World War early marriage had also been discouraged; they needed to have reached maturity and demonstrated 'steadiness' before the army would give any union its blessing. This meant that some soldiers who were marching to war in 1914 delayed marriage until their forties; while a few, as in one instance recounted in this book, created considerable difficulties for themselves by attempting to hide the fact that they were married at all.

Nevertheless, the surge of voluntary enlistment, which expanded the army to a hitherto undreamt-of size, and the subsequent introduction of conscription in January 1916, changed everything. The army's ranks were filled with five million civilians in uniform, serving for the duration of the war only. These were mostly young men, debating whether it was better to marry their sweethearts now or to wait until the war was over. Teddy and Molly Murphy had this discussion. So too did Sid Edwards and Kiddie Goodall. With death an ever-present possibility, the combat soldier's eternal conundrum remained the same: whether it was better to delay marriage and avoid the risk of leaving one's loved one a widow, or to marry immediately and have – as an optimist would put it – something to live for instead.

As the First World War continued, the insatiable demands of the army for more recruits meant that, from May 1916, married men as well as bachelors were conscripted. For the likes of William Harper, caught up in the widening net, the hardships of the trenches made them appreciate family life all the more. Where there were children involved, there is often an added poignancy to the correspondence, even more so when the letters themselves were addressed to a child. Such letters, as readers will discover, invariably prove charming, in spite of the often trying circumstances under which they were written.

Many letters in this book were written at times of danger, and we cannot deny the frisson that this gives us when we read them; love letters written by those in other walks of life seem tame by comparison. Most powerful of all are the 'last letters' to be read in the event of death. Fortunately, neither of the two examples included here were needed for that purpose, but there are instances where wives and fiancées did hear the worst, and these cases are never anything but moving.

On other occasions, wives and sweethearts endured the suspense of being out of contact with their soldier loves for prolonged periods. Sometimes not knowing what fate had befallen them was almost as bad as hearing the worst. This was particularly the case after Japan entered the Second World War in 1941; the war in the Far East was inherently remote, and with

British troops mounting a desperate defence in Singapore and Burma news, as Margaret Newman back in England discovered, was doubly hard to come by. But while the retreat through Burma proved exacting enough for her husband Harold, for others captured at Singapore the nightmare was only just beginning. The prisoner of war experience constitutes a whole sub-section of soldiers' letters, and for those like Ted Senior and Alan Glendinning, who both endured extreme privation at the hands of the Japanese, solace was sought in writing poetry, recollecting past happiness with their loved ones, and looking forward with eager anticipation to their reunion.

When the Second World War began in 1939, Britain was a very different society to what it had been twenty-five years before at the commencement of the First. The status of women, in particular, had been transformed, a process that Reg Bailey had jokingly commented upon to Hilda Gower when he heard in 1918 that they had received the vote. By the Second World War, soldiers' sweethearts like Valerie Erskine Howe and Joan Pendlebury were often themselves in uniform as members of the Auxiliary Territorial Service. This assertion of independence meant that men like Len Fletcher could not now expect their wives to sit moping at home while they were away for years on end; nonetheless, the freedom that Susan Fletcher enjoyed in her social life caused Len untold anguish as he came to realize the temptations being dangled in front of her.

For such reasons, the fear of infidelity raised its head to a greater extent during the Second World War. The presence of American troops in the United Kingdom did not help; Britain felt almost like a country under occupation and its womenfolk's heads seemed in danger of being turned. Nazi propaganda glee-fully seized upon the resentment felt towards American GIs by some British soldiers serving overseas. This though was simply a reversal of what the British soldier himself had experienced in the past, when he was the one who went to foreign countries and, on occasion, enjoyed himself with the locals. Moreover, there were echoes of this in the experiences of Tony Upfill-Brown and Cecil May in liberated Belgium, and of Nigel Gunnis in Romania. Romances 'in theatre', however, were not going to be written about in letters to sweethearts at home – if there was one – so these are documented in diaries such as Cecil May's or, perhaps surprisingly, in letters to soldiers' mothers.

Some letters written by soldiers in action reveal traces of a knight errant complex, in which deeds are dedicated to the war-rior's inamorata. John Rhodes considered the fact that he was 'an A1 man' and first-line combatant nothing less than his beloved deserved; while Peter Robinson professed that his award of the Military Medal had been inspired by his sweetheart.

However, it was under just these sorts of circumstances that soldiers risked becoming too intense, alienating the women to whom they wrote. It is striking that the most passionate letters, full of high-blown sentiments, often appear to have proved counterproductive. Indeed, so extreme and unexpected were the infatuated soldiers' declarations that in two instances included here they seem almost to have created an allergic reaction, the objects of veneration not only rejecting their suitors but never getting married at all.

Consequently, for those who may look for romantic inspira-tion within these pages, the message perhaps should be that humour is the best tactic. Reg Bailey's letters are self-deprecating and tongue-in-cheek throughout, but he gets the girl in the end. Similarly, May Utton's comic postcards, embellished with cheeky messages, are immensely appealing and provide an object lesson in how to keep fresh a relationship when someone is hundreds of miles away. Most tellingly of all though, Valerie Erskine Howe's distinctive humour persuaded Anthony Ryshworth-Hill that he should marry her.

It is fitting to conclude this Introduction on an upbeat note if only because, more by accident than design, and in spite of occasional misunderstandings, the sentiment expressed by the old saying *amor vincit omnia* ('love conquers all') emerges intact – if somewhat battered – in the pages that follow. The validity of this observation is perhaps confirmed by the fact that only in a single instance, because of the story's sensitivity, has it been deemed advisable to change the names of the principals concerned.

THE FIRST WORLD WAR

1914–1918

EDWARD AND ETHIE DE SALIS

When Great Britain declared war on Germany on 4 August 1914, joining the European conflagration that became known as the First World War, the mobilization of its small regular army to the Continent proceeded smoothly: pre-war staff planning had been excellent. At Mons on 23 August the 80,000 men of the British Expeditionary Force (BEF), led by Sir John French, encountered the German First Army, swinging through Belgium in an endeavour to outflank the defences of Britain's ally, France. Although the initial German assault was checked, the danger of being overwhelmed by superior numbers meant the BEF had to retreat. That this retirement was then successfully accomplished – largely due to the efforts of General Sir Horace Smith-Dorrien of II Corps – was hailed as a triumph. Among those back in England who thought so was Emily Ethel 'Ethie' de Salis. In 1902 she had married the then newly promoted 28-year-old Captain Edward de Salis of the Worcestershire Regiment, quickly proving herself the perfect army wife. Interested in her husband's career and anticipating, twelve years later, that a short European war – the common view was that it would be over by Christmas – would lead to his advancement, she wrote to Edward from Tidworth on 2 October 1914, informing him how she was keeping abreast of war news through the pages of the *Daily Mail*, and confided her expectation that the pressure exerted on the Germans by Britain's 'hairy hatted' Russian allies, as well as Britain's own Indian Army (the 'Sons of Ind'), would lead to speedy victory:

'Yours of the 25th just come. You write me a splendid description of the great retirement. By Jove it ought to be painted. I wonder if you know – that retreat was considered one of the finest *things our Army has ever done! They say no other troops in the world could have done it, and it was largely effected by the moral effect you had on the Germans and their dislike of meeting you at close quarters with cold steel. What Sir J. French said in his dispatch about S. Dorrien was small to what S. D. said about you all, in a letter to his wife. He said no troops but British could have stood what you did. That his divisions had pulled him out of what looked like inevitable disaster by courage, endurance, and initiative and you had done what he thought at the time was a human impossibility. I am following the campaign in the* Daily Mail *and keeping it all for you to read when you come home. As I told you before, we are kept in the dark – and only the most* obvious *news given. The Casualty list is not to be trusted ever and we have to go*

largely by intuition and knowing what is going on. You are well on the road to victory now and I am just waiting for the conflict in which our "hairy hatted" allies and our "Sons of Ind" are to take part. After that I expect to hear you are marching on Berlin! I expect it will be many months before we see one another again. Meantime you are doing your work for the King and Country and I am doing mine!'

Ethie's own work for king and country was to perform a pastoral role within her husband's regiment, looking after the welfare of the wives of other-rank soldiers. On 7 September, just as the successful French and British counterattack against the Germans was commencing on the River Marne, Edward still found time to write to her with advice: *'If you have any more trouble over the women write to Lady Smith-Dorrien. I understand she is running a fund and Miss Delmé Ratcliffe is Sec of it. We sent a sub of £25 before we left ... as for other Regts giving their married people money to carry on with, we hadn't a sou in our Canteen Fund.'*

Ethie replied cheerfully, reassuring Edward that the situation at the barracks at Tidworth was in hand: *'All the women are in their own homes now except Mrs Jarmold – her little son aged 5 days was born in hospital here and I am responsible for seeing her safely conveyed home. It has been a* tremendous *business looking after them ...'* She makes a curious observation about the wartime birth rate: *'Not a single girl baby has been born in the garrison since the declaration of war! Several infants have been born – officers' sons, and soldiers', but* all boys! *Everyone is much struck by the fact.'*

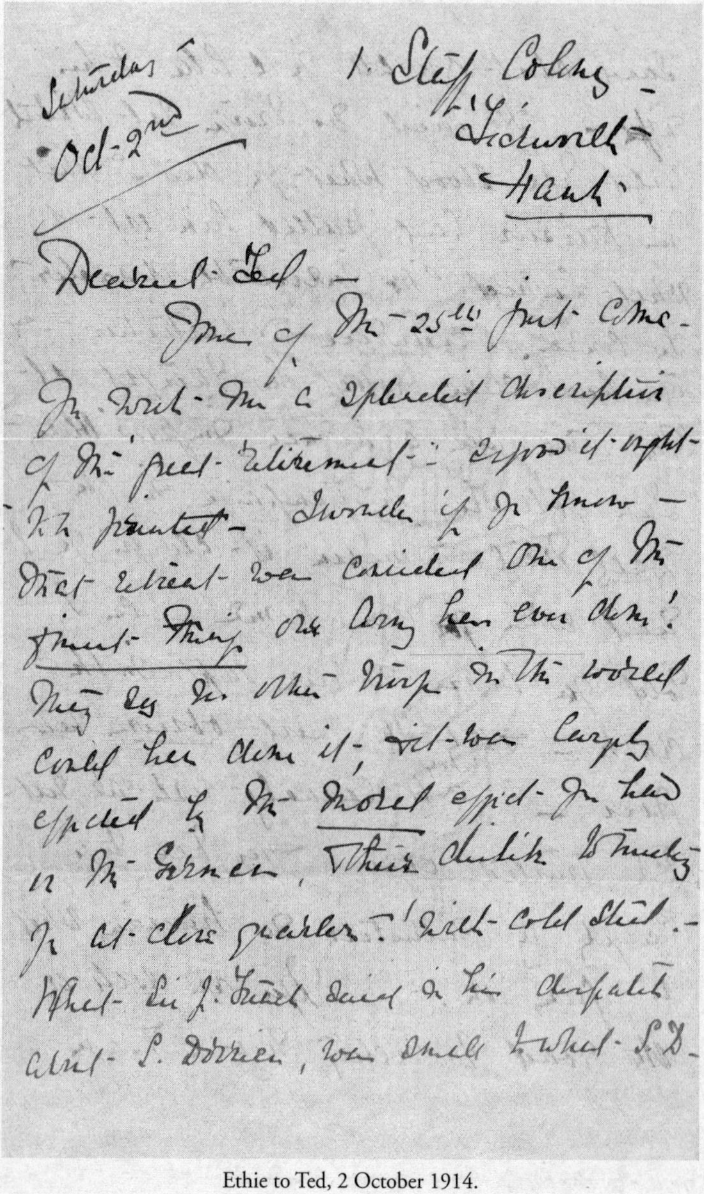

Ethie to Ted, 2 October 1914.

8 October. 1914.

Dearest Ethie.

The 12" anniversary of our
wedding day and only the 2nd we
have not spent together, the other
one was when I went back to the West
Indies alone; we have had some very
heavy marching lately, 17, 23, & 16
miles on three successive nights but
we have been away from shells, almost
out of sound of the guns for part of
the time which has been very pleasant.
Of course I can't say where we are
or what we are doing but you will
probably see it in the papers before
you get this letter. last night we
marched through a large town, which
had not been visited by Germans

Ted to Ethie, 8 October 1914.

On 8 October, Edward began a long letter to his wife by marking their wedding anniversary before digressing on the nature of war, how it was being reported and his own moments of excitement, punctuated by more practical concerns:

'The 12th Anniversary of our wedding day and only the second we have not spent together . . . We have had some very heavy marching lately: 17, 23, and 16 miles on three successive nights, but we have been away from shells and almost out of sound of the guns for part of the time, which has been very pleasant. Of course I can't say where we are or what we are doing but you will probably see it in the paper before you get this letter. Last night we marched through a large town, which had not been visited by Germans. It was very pleasant to see a town in full swing, with shops and streets all lighted up, the people all wandering about, without any fear on their faces. It had a tremendous effect on the men, who actually started to sing on the march again. English people, especially those actually living in England, don't know what war is – to them it is merely a word. In the homes where friends or relatives are lost it is only partly understood; but it is different over here, especially in those parts where the tide has swept along, or where there is a chance of it doing so. Even the animals show it in their faces: it is horrible to see the fear in the eyes of the dogs and horses – but such things are too beastly to write about.

. . . I got a parcel from home the other day, a pair of socks, some cigarettes, a pipe, some soap . . . We hear that our 100lbs of kit has gone back to Southampton so I have no spare kit here. Did you get my card asking for pants and boots, etc.? Brown K boots size eight

An Uhlan horse captured from the Germans, September 1914.

would do. Please have lips put on the toes and heels as they wear out so thin on these roads ... a couple of long sleeve vests would also be very nice, and some mitts as it is very cold now, especially when the sun is down in the morning. It will be awful later on if this goes on, which I still doubt. I may be optimistic but I don't think the war will last another month. I sincerely hope not. I have got a very nice Uhlan blanket from the kit of an Uhlan the company bagged when on outpost. It has a certain amount of blood on it but that can't be helped; it will be useful later on in the cold weather. I will tell you about that show when we get home: he nearly got me, as I thought he was one of our own cavalry. It was getting dark, he had a shot at me at 150 yds, I was standing in the middle of the road, expecting the General and 3 Cavalry men, and I took the 3 Uhlans for the Cav. I had no idea there were any Germans anywhere near us – fortunately Germans are not good shots! Well, dearest love to all.'

In June 1915, after much arduous service, Edward was transferred from regimental duties to the BEF's General Headquarters at Montreuil-Sur-Mer. From here he regaled Ethie with stories, some a little risqué:

'I always go to a tea shop called De Heran. It is rather a superior place and most filled with staff officers: Hobson told me it is called the Staff College. I have been to the Normandie two or three times, but it is usually crowded with young officers from the Base Depots and with "Ladies". One of our men was having dinner the other night and a "Lady" sent him a note. It was a very hot night; our fellow wrote on the back of the note, "I'm too old, besides it's a d— sight too hot!"'

In January 1916, as an acting lieutenant-colonel, Edward took command of the 9th Battalion of the Worcestershire Regiment in Mesopotamia, fighting the Turks. He led from the front and paid the price on 5 April 1916 during the abortive attempts to relieve the beleaguered British garrison at Kut, as he wrote to Ethie seventeen days later from a hospital bed in Bombay after evacuation to India:

'Hope my wire didn't worry you (I have a feeling you haven't got it yet). I sent it on Wednesday so that you should have got it in time to address your letter here, hence the "Express" mail and not a deferred one. I bust up the ankle in the big fight on the 5th, but

stuck it for 6 ½ hours, when it became so bad I was done – we lost 24 officers out of 28! All *the seniors, nothing but 3 Lieuts and the Quartermaster left!'*

Fortunately, Edward made a full recovery and finished the war in 1918 in command of a machine gun battalion. He retired from the army in 1923.

Frank and Emily Ryan

⸎

On 5 August 1914 Private Frank Ryan, a reservist who had left the army two years before, was recalled to the colours. A mere seventeen days later he was in France. As a horse driver in the Army Service Corps he served with the 10th Field Ambulance, which was attached to the 4th Division. When he wrote his first surviving letter to his wife, Emily, from Metren in Belgium on 15 October 1914, he did so to reassure her that he was well. The 4th Division had been engaged in heavy hand-to-hand fighting and the 10th Field Ambulance was stretched to the limit. The 'wounded were coming in fast', the unit war diary reported, and 'most of the wounds were of a severe nature due to the short range at which they were received'. Routine censorship nevertheless prevented Frank telling Emily anything of this: '*I would like to tell you a few of my experiences out here, but we must not say anything in our letters in case they read them and then they would not let them go through the post.'*

Frank's letters are full of the concerns and preoccupations of the majority of soldiers in the early stages of the war. Initially, he yearns hopelessly to return home at the end of the year: *'I live in hopes that the war will soon be over. I should like to be able to get home for Xmas but I very much doubt it.'* Around this time British soldiers and civilians alike were waking up to the fact that the war was not going to be the quick victory many had expected. Many First World War soldiers were worried too about how their families would cope financially while they were away fighting; and Frank Ryan, who harboured a guilty secret, had more reason to worry than most. Anxiously, he asked Emily if she was receiving the correct 'stoppage' from his wages:

'Are you getting your separation allowance alright? Only some of the fellows' wifes [sic] *has had a difficulty in getting it. And how do you go about drawing it? You know what I mean love. They stop me 6d* [sixpence] *a day which is compulsory stoppage since you come entitled to it, but I don't care if they stop the lot as long as I know you get it alright, because I know things must be dear to buy at home and I know you can do with it having Baby as well.'*

A portion of a married soldier's wages was automatically deducted from the amount he received and went straight to his wife, the amount varying depending on the number and age of the children in the family. So what had Frank Ryan to worry about?

Frank had married Emily Jane Hopwood in 1905, aged seventeen. He was a farm labourer who, because of the agricultural depression, had been out of work for a considerable time by May 1909. Like many before him in similar circumstances he decided to join the army. The problem, however, was that he was married, and married men were not eligible to enlist. This prohibition Frank decided to ignore, covering his tracks by enlisting under his stepfather's name, rather than his own, Dymond.

When he was recalled to the army in 1914, he was too frightened to come clean. By the autumn of 1915, the authorities eventually noticed that his wife's name was different to his own and confronted him. In a statement, he explained that his wife had suffered a serious scalding incident shortly before war broke out and, reluctant to risk undermining her health further by admitting his past deception and courting punishment, he had continued to serve under a false name.

In the event, Frank escaped sanction. He had returned from France in July 1915; the requirement to wear a surgical boot on his right foot meant that he was no longer fit for overseas service. He continued in the army until March 1919, achieving a medical discharge.

ANDREW AND DEENEY THORNE

As some soldiers' letters demonstrate, sweethearts could not only be grown women but beloved daughters. In the autumn of 1914, Andrew Thorne of the Grenadier Guards was a staff captain with the 1st Guards Brigade. Not yet thirty, he was of independent means and, notwithstanding the demands of his army career, had been able to marry young. He already had four children, three boys and a girl. The eldest of them was Diana, born in 1910; the youngest Peter, born on 6 August 1914, two days after war commenced.

Even during the heaviest fighting of the early months of the First World War Andrew wrote letters for Diana's mother, Margaret, to read to her. His own father had died when Andrew was sixteen, leaving him to become a surrogate father to his three younger sisters. His long experience of how to relate to

Andrew Thorne.

young girls is evident in the beautifully judged letters he sent to Diana, or 'Deeney' as she was known.

On 10 November 1914, as the First Battle of Ypres – which saw the BEF sacrifice itself to prevent the Germans pushing through to the Channel ports – was drawing to a close, Andrew did what he did so often, writing about the different types of animals he had encountered, including a playful kitten adopted by Brigade Headquarters:

'My dear Deeney,

Thank you and the boys so much for your letters. I do like getting
them and the funny little pictures as well. Also I think the sweeties
and chocs you choose for Dad are so nice. I wonder how you guessed
he liked barley sugar and the Suchard chocolate. Even the General
had some and he liked it too. It must be fun for you to have Mum
and Peter back at Highfield ... It does seem funny that poor Dad
hasn't any idea of what Peter looks like. Mum has sent Dad some
photos of you all, including Peter, but it is difficult to realize exactly
what he is like just by a photo ...

Did I ever tell you of the little kitten that we have adopted. We
found it about 10 days ago in an empty cottage – she was a grey
and seemed very fond of us so that we used to feed her. Then when
we had to leave, Serg[eant] Major took her away in his pocket. We
only stayed in the house for 2 or 3 days and then had to leave again,
so again the pussycat came in the pocket of the greatcoat. She lives
in the one remaining room of the farm – nearby where we have dug
ourselves underground – and plays with us when we have breakfast and dinner and when we wash and shave. Fancy, we only wash
once a day and that is at eleven o'clock at night. Bines gives the
kitten some milk, some bully beef and sometimes a sardine or two
so that she doesn't do badly. We used to get a lot of milk from 3 cows
at this farm but a cruel shell came and killed all the cows and about
ten pigs as well. Now we have to get the milk from a long way away.
All the houses and farms have been left by the owners and nearly all
of them have been destroyed or partly so by the shells from our and
the German guns. It does sound wicked, doesn't it!

I wonder how you all go out for walks now. Do you all go in

Margaret Thorne (left) with Deeney (right) and her
brothers in the goat cart.

*prams or has Peter been given one yet? Then I suppose you walk a
great deal or else have rides in Biddy's carriage. I did think Biddy*
[their goat] *looked well in the photo . . .*

*I hope you will really look after Mum and keep her ever so happy
and well. You see she will want a lot of help looking after three boys,
won't she? Give Mum a very big kiss from me and the same to the
boys. With best love from Dad.'*

As Andrew reported in another letter to Deeney, however, there
was alarm three days later when the kitten went missing. '*We are
in a very big home and perhaps she has gone to sleep in a corner
somewhere upstairs to get away from the shells which make such a
loud noise.*' But then, relief: '*The Sergt. Major has just come in to
tell me that she has been found. Last night she jumped on to the
Sergt. Major's face while he was asleep. He jumped up with a start*

Andrew Thorne (second right) at the front, October 1914.

and seized his revolver to do "a shoot, bang, fire" at a German and then all he saw was the kitten. She does eat a lot of bacon fat when we have it at breakfast. She will get too fat if she is not properly dieted.'

When Andrew wrote to Deeney on 27 November, he made reference to his horse, Punch, as well as a new pony. The latter was a replacement for his other horse, Judy, which had been killed underneath him at the height of the fighting at Gheluvelt on 31 October; although this had not prevented Andrew saving the day by carrying the message which famously brought the 2nd Worcestershire Regiment into the line.

'Poor Punchie has still got a little cold and is rather stiff, so he is rubbed every day like George was last spring when he was ill. I hope

Punchie will soon be well enough to be ridden. My new little brown pony is such a nice little one – he is rather naughty as he pretends to be frightened of everything he passes on the road but he doesn't really mean to be naughty. I think he used to be driven in a pony trap. I wonder if there were any little girls or boys he used to draw behind him. If he doesn't get killed, I must try and arrange to buy him off the government and have him at Farnborough Park.'

The weather was now getting cold and snow lay on the ground, giving Andrew scope to paint one of his most felicitous verbal pictures. '*When I arrived here last Tuesday, I thought I must be almost silly as I saw, instead of men, what looked like polar bears, brown bears, and black bears walking about in our billets; I was*

Punch (left) and Judy.

almost frightened. Fortunately I quickly found my Sergeant Major who explained that all the men had been given fur coats for the winter and they were trying them on. The coats are not like Uncle Tommie's with the fur inside but like Mum's black one with the fur outside.'

Andrew had the knack of being able to convey a sense of the devastation around him in terms Deeney would be able to understand: '*All the little children have left this village a long time ago, as the Germans used to put shells into their houses and smash them up like the Boys did when they got into your doll's house.*' He let his daughter know in a playful fashion that he was moving in lofty circles: '*Daddy at this moment is eating a big bullseye that Lord Normanby sent him. The other day some Generals came to see Daddy's General and they were all given big bullseyes with the result that no one spoke at all for about ten minutes, the sweets were so big.*'

He knew, too, how to make Deeney metaphorically shiver. On 8 January 1915, he told her how he performed his ablutions: '*The soldiers are so dirty and muddy here that they have to clean themselves with petrol, like one does clothes. Dad had to have his bath in the back yard and stood under the pump while his servant pumped the water all over him. It was so cold!*'

Andrew Thorne continued to write regularly to Deeney for the rest of the war, which saw him rise first to command a battalion and then a brigade. Between the wars he was a British military attaché in Berlin. On one occasion he found himself summoned to discuss the Battle of Gheluvelt with Adolf Hitler, who had discovered that they had both fought there (and been, it was decided, within 200 yards of each other). Afterwards, during the Second World War, he was General Officer Commanding in Scotland.

Andrew Thorne died in 1970. His daughter Diana, who rose to be a colonel in the Women's Royal Army Corps, lived on until 1983.

Deeney went on to join the forces herself in the Second World War, as did most of her family. Here she is standing, left, in 1940. Andrew is seated in front of her.

Arthur and Florence
Harrington

Arthur Harrington, a regular soldier attached as Regimental Sergeant-Major to the London Rifle Brigade (part of the Territorial Force, which in peacetime was made up of part-time soldiers), left behind his pregnant wife Florence Margaret Harrington and their young daughter Margaret when he departed for France with the BEF in late 1914. Arthur came from a military family: he fought in the Boer War with the King's Royal Rifle Corps (KRRC), receiving the Distinguished Conduct Medal, and his father and five brothers also fought with the KRRC.

In his letters home from the First World War, he constantly wrote about how much he missed his wife and daughter: '*You and my darling child are constantly in my thoughts ... God bless you both, my dearie, and keep you well till I can enfold you in my arms again.*' He wrote to his wife regularly, telling her about his journey to and arrival in France; the training undergone by the brigade on arrival in marching, shooting, and constructing trenches; that he had plenty of food, was fit and sleeping well; that he missed newspapers very much and had no idea what was going on at the front.

As the Brigade worked their way towards the front line and entered the trenches, he wrote about the cold, the noise of the guns, the lack of sleep, and how difficult life was in the open trenches: '*The men whom the LRB* [London Rifle Brigade] *relieved last night didn't look much like the British soldier one is accustomed to see, with their clothing all plastered with mud, their matted hair and beards, and dirty faces. Poor fellows, they have had a rough time indeed ever since the war commenced. It is probably a fortnight or more since they were able to wash themselves.*'

Arthur's letters reveal just how desperately he missed his wife and daughter during the winter of 1914: '*You are both being thought of by me constantly. I think of you when I lie down at night, on rising in the morning, whilst on the march – in fact in all my waking hours and only hope that you are both as fit and well as myself at the present moment . . . Kiss my darling daughter for her Daddy, who would love to get hold of her, and with fondest love to yourself.*' On another occasion he wrote: '*She [Margaret] must know that her Daddy constantly thinks of her and her mother and that he looks forward to the day, though that may be some distance off, when he will be able to take both of them in his arms again.*'

Florence meanwhile sent him a picture of herself and their daughter. In the letter which Arthur wrote to thank her for the

Arthur Harrington in the uniform of the King's Royal Rifle Corps,
wearing his Boer War medals, the DCM among them.

photo – '*It is now my chief treasure in actual possession*' – he mentioned that his Brigade had suffered their first fatality: '*We lost our first man yesterday. Killed by a shell.*' Arthur was also concerned that his family keep up their spirits despite their separation: '*The style and tone of your letters assure me that you are keeping well and bright, and that is the condition I desire above all others that you should always find yourself in, so that I may find the same happy girl awaiting me on my return as I left behind. Keep my petlet well, too, please, because her Daddy is going to have some big games with her when he gets back.*'

In his letters to his wife at the close of 1914, Arthur wrote of the good food the Brigade enjoyed over Christmas, and thanked her for the Christmas pudding she sent him. He asked her to buy herself a Christmas box from him. In early 1915, he wrote of the endless wet weather, the water in the trenches and the mud everywhere, of the inactivity and repetition, of his farmhouse billet, and of the Brigade's desire to move forward. He often asked for reassurance that she and Margaret were well, that they were cheerful, and coping financially. He asked them not to worry about him. As her pregnancy advanced, his letters revealed his increasing concern for her well-being: '*Above all things, my dearest,*' he wrote, '*fight against the feelings of loneliness and depression which I know must assail you at times . . .*'

At the end of January, Arthur briefly returned home on leave to visit his now heavily pregnant wife. His letters to her on his return to the front are extremely tender. In one particularly romantic and moving letter, written in early March 1915, he openly wrote of his love for her:

'*The frequent expressions of your tender love for me touch me very deeply. It is indeed a comfort to me always that you are able to say that your life during the last three years, since we were happily united at the altar, has been a happy one. It is only what you deserve, dearest, for you have been a model wife and I have plenty of reason to bless the day you became my wife and true helpmeet. Please God many happy days together are still in store for us, at least such will be the case if any efforts of mine avail. I crave for you and my Margaret so often but must be like many other men out here in being patient.*'

His letters from this period were also deeply concerned with Florence's impending delivery: '*When you are able to inform me that you have been safely delivered, dearest, my mind will be very considerably relieved ... You are constantly in my thoughts. I only*

While Arthur was encamped at Bisley, Surrey, in September 1914, Florence paid him a visit.

wish it were possible to be with you and to be able to bear some of the pain when your time comes.' As her due date came closer, so his letters became more frequent: *'As it isn't possible to be with you, to allow me to try to cheer and comfort you in your hour of trial I have determined to send a brief epistle each day until it is over, in the hope that you may derive some little solace and support from same.'*

Arthur finally received the news he had been waiting for on 14 April 1915. Florence had safely given birth to a baby girl, whom they decided to christen Joan:

'The wire announcing your safe delivery reached me yesterday evening at 6 o'clock. You scarcely need to be told how glad I was to get the intelligence of your having had a satisfactory time and that all had gone well ... Of course when you feel well and strong enough you must send me a full description of the new arrival ... Don't on any account be in a hurry to leave your bed. I know you will desire to be there as short a time as possible but getting up too quickly might only result in your having to return there.

Well, darling, thank God you are alright ... Give my love to Bert, please. Heaps of love to you and "le petite fille" from your loving hubby, Arthur.'

Tragically, just two weeks later, on 28 April, Arthur was killed by an exploding shell while eating breakfast. He was forty-six years old, and had been married to Florence for only three years. He is commemorated at Ypres on the Menin Gate Memorial.

Two weeks after his death, Florence received a letter which must have made her very proud. It was written from the

Orderly Room of the London Rifle Brigade at Haywards Heath (the signature on the letter is illegible) on 9 May.

'My dear Mrs Harrington

I could not, during the first few days of your terrible anguish, intrude upon you with a letter, but I may now ask you to accept my most heartfelt sympathy. Your dear husband was a very, very, dear friend of mine and his loss to us all is absolutely irreparable. Deeply as I had learnt to admire his many grand qualities in the old days, I discovered even more during the first two months of mobilization when I was so closely associated with him. At each of our stopping places he looked after me like the real friend he was, taking me to the same billets as he had, and letting me share his tent at Bisley and Crowborough. His companionship was truly delightful and a most marvellous foil to the miserable treatment I received from the "heads".

We have lost many old friends and had many shocks, but none has been such a terrible blow to us all. Even those men who, less fortunate than I, knew him only slightly, are terribly grieved, and I can assure you that the heart of every member of the LRB goes out to you in your time of trial. My wife has told me how bravely you receieved the news; may your bravery remain with you.

Please let me know at any time if the Regiment can do anything for you as we shall all look upon it as a privilege to do anything that our dear old Sergeant Major would have wished . . .'

REGINALD AND ELEANORE STEPHENS

❧

Lieutenant-Colonel Reginald Stephens, a 45-year-old veteran of wars against the Sudanese Dervishes and the Boers, commanded the 2nd Battalion the Rifle Brigade in northern France during the winter of 1914–15. On 20 February he invited an old comrade in arms, Brigadier-General John Gough VC, to visit the trenches of the battalion in which he had once served. Gough was a rising star in the British military firmament, chief of staff to Sir Douglas Haig of 1st Army, and about to take command of a division. As the pair of them approached the trenches by a road 200 yards behind the front line, a shot rang out. A German sniper, nearly three-quarters of a mile away on Aubers Ridge, succeeded in badly wounding Gough.

Stephens was shaken: Gough was a friend and he felt

Eleanore and Reginald Stephens.

responsible. At a moment like this he needed someone in whom he could confide, and there was no one better than his wife of the past ten years, Eleanore Dorothea. To her, the mother of his three children, Stephens could explain his anguish:

'My darling

Alas a disaster and I'm broken hearted. Johnnie Gough came up here today and was shot in the stomach. They've taken him away to Estaires and as luck will have it, Sir A[rthur] Bowlby, the great surgeon, is there so poor Johnnie will have every chance. But it is a bad wound, how bad we don't know, as our doctor did not examine him closely as it is everything not to move him about. But my dear I feel as if it was my fault. I asked him to come to see the Battalion. I went to meet him and brought him what I thought was the safest way. He said he wanted to look at the ridge in front of us and we stopped a moment on the road side. It was then he was shot. Oh my darling I'm so sad about it. I ought to have known better, I suppose. But it's a road we use every day and all day. It was very quiet and I wasn't dreaming of danger. Oh my dear I can't forgive myself.

I've written to Mrs Johnnie and I've wired to Hubert [Gough, John's brother]. *You might write again to Mrs Johnnie as mine went off some hours ago in hopes of catching the King's Messenger. Since then they've taken him away from here. When he went he was under morphia but conscious and his condition was satisfactory; pulse good and he'd recovered from the shock.*

. . . Goodbye now my darling. I'm sorry for so sad a letter but I do feel it dreadfully. I get pretty callous about these things but

My darling

Alas a disaster & I'm broken hearted. Johnnie Gough came up here today and was shot in the stomach. They've taken him away to Estaires and as luck will have it Sir A Bowlby the great surgeon is there so poor Johnnie will have every chance. But it is a bad wound, how bad we don't know as our doctor did not examine him closely as it is everything not to move him about. But my dear I feel as if it was my fault. I asked him to come & see the Butt: I went to meet him and brought him what I thought was the safest way. He said he wanted to look at the ridge in front of us and we stopped a moment on the road side. It was then he was shot. Oh my darling I'm so sad about it. I ought to have known better I suppose. But it's a road we use every day & all day. It was very quiet and I wasn't dreaming of danger. Oh my dear I can't forgive myself.
I've written to Mrs Johnnie and I've wired to Herbert you might wire again to Mrs Johnnie as mine went off some hours ago in hopes of catching the King's messenger. Since then they've taken him away from here. When he went he was under morphia but conscious & his condition was satisfactory quite good & he'd recovered from the shock.
No letters or papers got here yesterday owing to the change of time of the boats, we think, due to submarines. They are to sail at night. Aldridge is

'Alas a disaster …' The letter Reginald wrote on the wounding of Johnnie Gough.

this is above a bit. Goodbye my darling. My love to the dear smalls.

Ever your loving
Stiff' [His army nickname was 'Stiff 'Un']

But lingering hopes for John Gough were soon dashed:

'Poor Mrs Johnnie came over but was too late. He died at 5 a.m. and she arrived about ten. The Battalion buried him in Estaires cemetery in the afternoon. I saw poor Mrs Johnnie and gave her his messages but it was heart breaking and I was very sad. Everyone has been very kind to me and says I am not in anyway to blame, but it is dreadfully on my conscience. I suppose I ought to have done different, but how I don't know. I saw Sir A. Bowlby who with another big man operated and they say there was no chance from the first. They say it was a ricochet, which I didn't think, but the bullet went in at the side and travelled round inside him, lodging behind his spine. Now my dear I can't talk about it any more.'

If Stephens needed to unburden himself to Eleanore on this occasion, within three weeks he would need to do so again. Apart from re-acquainting himself with old friends, a second reason motivating John Gough to visit Stephens' battalion had been to undertake a personal reconnaissance of the German positions in preparation for a British offensive. This was launched on 10 March 1915 at Neuve Chapelle, with the 2nd Rifle Brigade in the van. Initially the attack was a success and Stephens' men took their objective. But success went unexploited. Stephens felt he could have pressed on, and whether he could have done so with any likelihood of breaking through has been debated by historians ever since. By the time he was allowed to advance German resistance had stiffened. After the failure of two costly attempts to attack Stephens had to take upon himself the awful responsibility of disobeying his orders to continue the assault. Writing to Eleanore, he was forthright; and although as a battalion commander no one would be censoring his letters, he felt it prudent at the end to write across the top of his missive *'I've said too much in parts of this. Don't repeat.'*

'March 14

My very dear heart

We've had no end of a time and we've lost sadly, but my dear I am unhurt so far and still have every intention of returning to you when it is all over. We had a great success at first and took the village of Neuve Chapelle and a lot of Germans. It was a really good show and I'm very proud of the Battalion. After that things went wrong. We wanted to go on and could have easily. We really had a hole right through their lines and there was nothing in front of us. But the people on our left failed because their artillery couldn't or didn't hit the enemy's wire. Consequently we were stopped and not allowed to proceed.

That was on Thursday. On Friday morning we were ordered to go on as the people on our left were thro' but by that time the Germans had dug themselves in and we failed, losing heavily. At 5 p.m. we tried again, losing badly again. I was so angry, I knew it was impossible but I was ordered to try again, regardless of loss; it was a dreadful position to be put in. The thing was manifestly impossible: 500 yds of deep plough and machine guns in front and on both flanks. Our men didn't gain 200 yards and those that went were simply wiped out. I stopped it after a few had gone out and went back and chucked in my hand and said I would not give any further order to advance. (This my dear is for your own ears alone). It was a dreadful situation and I suppose I might have been tried for cowardice, but saner counsels prevailed and the thing was stopped.

Meanwhile we lost 12 officers and over 300 men, but I feel that I saved a remnant, for we should all have been killed and no ground gained. All this because of a muddle in the artillery fire at the beginning on our left. It was rather sad; so near being a big thing. The hole was almost made, in fact it was made and we only wanted the word to go forward and troops could have poured thro' after us, but it never came. As our left failed I suppose it was right to stop the right or we'd have been "in the air", but it is very sad to have done your part and then to be put in the soup because others fail.

… Now I must stop my darling, a man is waiting to take this. Goodbye my dearest, I give many thanks for coming thro all right and pray so to see you again. Goodbye my darling. Ever yr loving Stiff.'

ELEANORE STEPHENS
AND THE WIVES OF THE
2ND RIFLE BRIGADE

Neuve Chapelle was no blot on Stephens' record and he had risen to be a corps commander by the war's end. While he no doubt never forgot being a direct witness to the dreadful slaughter of Neuve Chapelle, in a strange way it was perhaps his wife who was exposed to a greater extent to the heartache that such loss could cause. Eleanore Stephens at the time managed the 2nd Rifle Brigade's comforts fund, arranging for warm clothing and off-ration foodstuffs to be distributed among its soldiers. She became a trusted figure among the soldiers' wives and it was only natural that in the wake of Neuve Chapelle they should turn to her for news of their husbands. There is great pathos in their anxious letters.

'March 22 1915

Dear Mrs Stephens,

I hope you will forgive me troubling you, but I thought you might be able to tell me if the 2nd Batt Rifle Bde has been in action, for I have received no news of Mr Clark since the 9th and I am very much troubled about him, so I thought you would let me know. It would ease my mind, for I feel properly downhearted. Hoping your Husband is quite well and safe and your dear self, for this war is terrible.

   Yours truly
   Mary Clark'

For Mary Clark at least there would be relief.

'Wed 24 1915

Dear Mrs Stephens,

I received your kind letter, and am pleased to tell you I received news of Mr Clark. I got a p[ost] c[ard] and a letter dated 15th and 19th and they both came together this morning. He was quite well, so I am quite happy now and content. I think they have advanced well, and thank God for their victory. Hoping they all keep safe, with best wishes for you, and your Husband for Mr Clark said he was a Gentleman.

   Yours truly
   Mary Clark'

Mrs Edith Stevens was another who experienced the joy of knowing that her husband was alive.

'March 25 1915

Dear Madam

Thank you very much for your kind letter I received from you informing me about my husband. I was very worried and upset because I hadn't heard from him since he left for the trenches but I had a letter this morning telling me he is quite well and that he had just come out of the trenches until Monday. I do hope the war will soon end for everybody's sake especially those that have dear ones fighting for their Country. It is a terrible trying time especially when the children keep asking when their daddy is coming home. My poor Husband hasn't even seen our dear baby, he came home for a fortnight when he was wounded and had to return before she was born. She will be three months old on Sunday. I hope he will soon be home again with them . . . thanking you very much.

>*I Remain*
>*Yours very truly*
>*Mrs Edith Stevens'*

The suspense too was proving unbearable for Mrs Mary Mace:

'Dear Madam.

You will wonder why I am writing to you again, but I want to know if you can get to know off your husband about my husband as I have not heard off him for three weeks and I am very anxious about him as I have had my letters so regular up to now. The last time he wrote he told me his chest and throat were bad and I wonder if he has been taken worse ... perhaps you will tell me where I can get to know if you don't care to ask your husband. Dear Madam I thought with him being colonel he might know but I hope your husband is still safe. It makes us worry, we dont know half the poor things have gone through. I for one will be thankful when it is over and I am sure you will too. If I do get to know where my husband is I will let you know. You see I might hear before I get an answer from you. I will put my husband's full address and hope you will help me to get to know which I am sure you will by the kind letter you sent me a while ago.

Yours truly
Mary J. Mace

My husband's address
Rfn F Mace Z 923
A Company 2nd Batt. R.B.
25 Infantry Brigade
8th Division
Expeditionary Force'

In this instance there would be no happy ending. Rifleman Frank Mace was among those killed at Neuve Chapelle on 12 March 1915. He has no known grave.

Mrs Mace
25 rvale Rd
Darnall
Sheffield

Dear Madam.

You will wonder why I am writing to you again, but I want to know if you can get to know off your husband about my husband as I have not heard off him for three weeks and I am very anxious about him. as I have had my letters so regular up to now. the last time he wrote he told me his chest and throat were bad. and I wonder if he has been taken worse. but it is so

One of the many letters Eleanore Stephens received asking for her help in tracing news of missing husbands

James and Nan Walmsley

Sergeant James Walmsley joined the Military Mounted Police (MMP) on 13 February 1915. Six-foot, dark-haired and blue-eyed, James had previously joined the Royal Horse Guards at the age of eighteen, serving four and a half years before buying his discharge in order to join the civilian police. On 1 March 1915, now aged twenty-nine, he set sail for Egypt, leaving behind in Wantage, Berkshire, his wife Beatrice Annie, known as Nan, whom he had married in 1909. Once in Egypt, James joined an army being assembled to fight the Turks, who had joined the war on the side of Germany in October 1914.

James sent a series of postcards home to Nan from Alexandria, together with Christmas and New Year cards. The postcards are cheeky, light-hearted and full of jokes. In them he calls his wife 'duck' and 'duckie' and signs off 'Roll on'

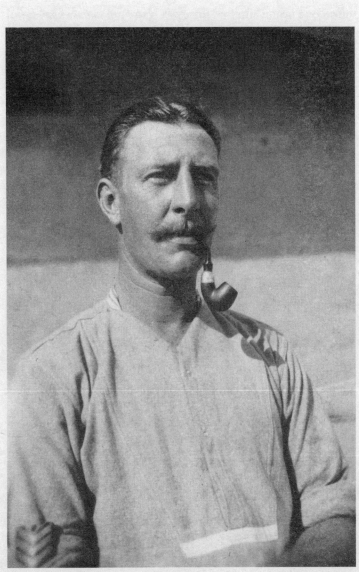

James Walmsley.

and 'Ta ta, my dear flower'. All of them are brief, a few lines at most; one begins simply, '*Excuse PC but I am so busy now, I can't write letter.*' But what makes them endearing is the obvious affection that shines through them: this is a couple who are clearly completely at ease with one another, such that a few words of what almost reads like a code between them was all they needed to reaffirm their love.

Walmsley was romantic, and the cards are written in charming and vivacious language; in one he wrote: '*look at the date above, I kissed your photo all over today*'. He tells her about the presents he is sending her: a string of beads and a brooch he has ordered specially, and he is immensely struck by the Alexandrian fashions: '*Very smart clothes worn here latest Paris fashions*'; '*It would please you to see the styles of dress here they are champion.*' In other cards he tells his wife about the plants and trees in the city, and makes recommendations as to what she should be putting in their allotment back at home. He often mentions the intense Egyptian heat: '*Hope you are in the pink duck. I am champion but oh so Hot XXX.*' He asks that she send him socks, but not any more Woodbines [cigarettes] as they make him cough.

James sent his wife a few other memorable items alongside the postcards, which she must have really treasured. One New Year he sent her a beautiful silk postcard, embroidered in blue with birds, flowers, and the message 'How I Miss You'. In 1919 he sent her a card from the YMCA in Jerusalem with a tiny bunch of dried flowers on the front, and the message 'Flowers from the Holy Land'. On other occasions, however, the appropriate card was evidently harder to find. At Christmas time in 1915 James was obliged to improvise, sending Nan the only festive-looking

Nan Walmsley.

item he could get his hands on, after writing 'MERRY XMAS' and drawing the badge of the MMP on it: *'Only Xmas card I could find – some Turkish General's luggage label – so madame, anyway, it's got a bit of red string on it.'*

Walmsley kept a diary from February 1915 to February 1916, also in the Museum's collection, which gives a factual account of his service in Egypt and Gallipoli. The Military Mounted Police were responsible for policing the British troops abroad, and James' diary gives a wonderful insight into his role and responsibilities.

'Fri 2.4.15. Good Friday, no difference very hot, went for ride round No.3 Camp ... thousands of French troops with mules

James and colleagues enjoying a rare moment of leisure from their duties with the Military Mounted Police.

*coming in, British Artillery also passing through. Stayed in camp
at night, arrested No. 2633 Pte Cecil Storey. R[oyal] A[rmy]
M[edical] C[orps] at Gabbria Camp, A. Canteen, for violent conduct to native at same place 9.30 p.m.'*

*'7.4.15 ... called out at 1.30 a.m. to quell disturbance at the
Moulin Rouge (Hotel) American Ship. Tennesse sailor (Battleship)
pulled knife out and threatened to stab me, held it near chest –
severe mauling? Not half.'*

James' diary reveals that he arrested men for drunkenness, for
stealing, and regularly broke up brawls. He also acted as an
escort for Turkish prisoners of war, and was often on duty at
the horse races in Alexandria. He recounts a memorable occasion when an Australian caused an immense disturbance in a
bar in the city by taking all the beer and refusing to pay. Like
his postcards, the diary entries often mention the tremendous
heat. They also record the everyday details of his life in various army camps and barracks; the mosquitoes, having his
hair cut, washday, bath day, writing to his wife, and even
planting cabbages in the ground around the barracks at Fort
Kom-el-Dik.

The tone of many of his entries is fairly light:

*'12.6.15 ... bought Bathing drawers (posh ones) Shaved moustache
off.'*

Once he was sent to take part in the Gallipoli Campaign in June
1915, however, the entries become increasingly gruesome:

'Tues 21.9.15. Myself, Clare, and Burgess ordered to go on top in view of Turks Trenches about 600 yds away to get kits Rifles and Bayonets off dead bodies, plenty of them too. I was in front B next and C behind carrying Rifles and Kit, Turk Sniper let fly went past my left cheek got Burgess right through the chest and back ... Rotten job taking webb Kit off dead men they fall to pieces, hundreds of both sides, most Turks.'

The Allies' unsuccessful campaign to land on the Gallipoli Peninsula and seize Constantinople from the Ottoman Empire had begun in April 1915. Both sides suffered huge casualties during the landings and initial attacks, and by the time James arrived in June the fighting had settled into trench warfare. Conditions were horrendous, and thousands died from disease and exposure. In December 1915, recognizing the futility of their position, the Allied forces began to withdraw from the Peninsula. The merry and loving tone of James' missives to his wife contrasts strongly with his graphic diary entries, and one can appreciate how hard he was trying to protect her from the grim reality of much of his service:

'Buck up old soul soon be back. Fondest from your Jim x'.

CHARLES AND KATHLEEN MELLISS

Although, after a glittering start, Major-General Charles Melliss' military career would end in disappointment, he had one consolation: he was able to express his frustrations – usually caused by the fellow generals with whom he had to work – to his wife. The daughter of a general herself, she could be expected to sympathize with his preoccupations, as the tenor of his letters to her during the First World War suggest.

As a 38-year-old major in the Indian Army, Melliss had won the Victoria Cross in West Africa in 1900, an exploit which established his reputation. A year later he married Kathleen Walter, fourteen years his junior. In March 1915 Melliss led the 30th Brigade from India to Mesopotamia (modern-day Iraq) to protect the oilfields around Basra against the Turks; during the victory won by General Sir John Nixon at Shaiba the following month Melliss played the leading part. His wife, working not entirely happily in a hospital in Alexandria (Egypt), wrote expressing her pleasure at his success, and Charles replied, alluding to the Germans' first use of poison gas at the Second Battle of Ypres shortly before:

'*I got your letter telling me you had heard the news of the battle of Shaiba through Younghusband, and am very pleased you are pleased and that the news bucked you up, for I could see by your letters that you were not feeling very perky. The hospital work must be depressing as well as tiring, seeing so many poor fellows suffering, but what must the gas poisoning be like; I am glad you don't see that. By Heaven I wouldn't spare a German if I got into a*

Kathleen (centre, seated) and Charles (second right, seated).

trench of them in command of a company . . . and I am glad to see
it looks as if our fellows are at last roused to real anger and hatred
of the swine . . .'

Unfortunately, as he also wrote to Kathleen, news of Shaiba
reached India too late to make him eligible for command of the
newly-formed 12th Division, which went instead to Major-
General George Gorringe. Charles had no problems with
Gorringe initially, but with others he could, as he admitted, let
rip: *'[Gorringe] seems a good sort of fellow but I can't stick Kennedy,*
who commands the cavalry, you remember him. He has the repu-
tation of being a most quarrelsome man, and it is a true one; but
unfortunately for him he met another person who can be equally
rude and aggressive when once roused, and I let him have a very
rough few minutes the other day.'

By June 1915 Kathleen clearly felt the strain of coping with the
influx of casualties now arriving at her hospital from the fighting at Gallipoli. Charles, writing from Basra, tried to raise her
spirits, but in the end could not prevent himself from implying
that he was perhaps more to be pitied, consigned to the back-
water of Mesopotamia while great things were happening at
Gallipoli: *'Don't let the hospital depress you. Remember they are*
lucky fellows to be fighting in such an important area of the great
war. It is we poor devils that deserve commiseration for we cannot
feel we are fighting for any good purpose.'

By now it had been decided by the Indian Government that
its army in Mesopotamia would take the offensive, push north
up the rivers Tigris and Euphrates to Amara and Nasiriyah

respectively, and create a greater buffer zone for the oilfields of Basra against the Turks. Charles, though, writing to Kathleen on 1 August, was unimpressed with the tactics employed by his divisional commander in capturing Nasiriyah: '*Why on earth Gorringe did not push on with the reserve brigade in ships straight on into Nasariyeh no one can say. He might have got the whole Turkish force to surrender; as it was they got clean away during the evening and night. It was extraordinary. He is a rotten General and we all felt a great lack of confidence in him ... It has been a veritable nightmare the last 3 weeks: he owes it to my advice that we did not have a reverse.*'

The following day, after Gorringe had blamed Melliss for entering Nasiriyah before him, Kathleen was once again the sounding-board of her husband's frustration: '*He sent me a snorter saying my action was subversive to discipline, etc. . . . I said I was absolutely unconscious of any intention to disregard his orders and requested him to withdraw his remarks. He refused, so I said I would refer the matter to Sir John Nixon, and sent him later a private note saying I wished our relationship in future to be purely official. The damned fellow has only been too glad of my support and advice during these last 3 weeks ... and indeed I played up to the swine and gave him my thorough cooperation. However I have asked and got a month's leave to India.*'

In a classic example of 'mission creep', it was now decided to occupy Kut, 160 miles further up the River Tigris from Amara. Kut having been captured at the end of September by General Charles Townshend's 6th Division, it was then decided that Baghdad, another 120 miles to the north, should be the next objective. To accomplish this goal, Townshend requested that he be joined by Melliss, newly returned from India.

Townshend's division was in reality too weak to reach Baghdad and it was repulsed at the Battle of Ctesiphon. After retreating back to Kut, Townshend and his men were surrounded by the Turks at the beginning of December 1915; the resulting siege of the town lasted for almost five months. During its course, Charles became as critical of Townshend as he had been of Gorringe before him. Writing a long letter in the form of a diary to Kathleen, his entry for Christmas Day was excoriating.

'*T[ownshend] is a hopeless incapable dreamer and ass, vain as a peacock and full of military history comparisons, but as a practical soldier one's grandmother would be as good. Sometimes one doesn't know whether to laugh or cry at his incapacity. He never goes near his men, or rarely – never goes near the front line of trenches and sees things for himself. But he is not the only rotter – there are several in high places. I tell you honestly K[athleen], although it sounds conceited for me to say it, but I can say it to you: I am the best man in this force of the senior Generals and what I suggest is accepted at once. It is not saying much though, but there are amongst the seniors an awful set of incompetents.*

Later. I have had a dinner of a tough goose and your plum pudding [which had arrived in one of the last parcels to reach Kut], *the latter very good . . .*'

Desperate attempts to relieve the garrison of Kut continued throughout the winter and spring of 1916. All failed. By 29

April, having run out of supplies, Townshend's force surrendered. For Charles this was a bitter pill. Captivity awaited him; his hopes of making a mark in the war were at an end.

'T sent in his formal surrender of Kut this morning. We have been destroying our guns and rifles, ammunition, etc., even my old revolver. We are to be moved on to camp some 5 miles upstream and evacuate Kut, but this is to be done in steamers – we couldn't walk; besides, we are shut in by floods. T is allowed on parole to Constantinople and hopes to get to London on parole and work on ransom. Lucky beggar anyhow to get out of this – of course I succeed him but am at present too seedy – the jaundice is still on me; I feel so rotten but am on the mend. It is so wretched to be ill at such a time. I feel I want to be up and at T's elbow, urging and advising though there is after all nothing to be done now – we are "in the

Receiving the last wireless message from Kut before it fell. This photograph was taken by a member of the relieving force.

soup"! I sent you a wireless [message] last night which I hope you will get, darling little K, to help cheer you up. My cloud has a silver lining – things perhaps may mend for me. Anyhow Khalil [the Turkish commander] *is a gentleman and says we shall be treated as their "most sincere and precious guests", as the Russians treated Osman Pasha after his glorious stand at Plevna [in 1877]. I hope I shall be able to get this letter to you somehow, darling girl. I have tried to get to Baghdad 3 times! It looks as if I were going to get there this time allright!! Later. We have hauled down our ragged old flag and hoisted the white flag. The Arabs are cheering in the town and a Turkish battalion is marching in to take over here, and so it is time, darling K, to write finis to the Siege of Kut. We have done our best.'*

Arthur and Euphemia Money

Arthur Wigram Money was born in 1866, and joined the Royal Artillery in 1885 at the age of nineteen. He had a varied and successful army career, serving mostly in India where he acted as Persian interpreter to the Commander-in-Chief from 1898 to 1900, and in South Africa during the Boer War where he acted as Assistant Adjutant General for Transport from 1900 to 1902. In March 1911, at the age of forty-five, a General Staff Officer at the War Office, Money married 29-year-old Euphemia Mabel Drummond in London. Their first child, David, was born in 1912. Later that year, the couple settled in India with their young son, where Money was now a Brigadier General with the General Staff. When the war broke out in 1914, Euphemia was pregnant with their second son, George, who was born in November that year in Calcutta. In early 1915 their eldest son, three year-old David, caught dengue fever and Euphemia returned to England with the two boys, leaving Arthur in India.

Arthur, a devoted husband and family man, was terribly lonely. He wrote to his wife every week, adding an instalment to his weekly letter almost every day. On Good Friday 1915, as Euphemia and the boys were sailing home, he wrote to her: '*Now I've had my solitary dinner, been reading on the verandah and then came in to read my little girl's letter again and have a little talk with her before going to bed . . . Darling I do want you so and feel very lonely tonight. All my love to you my own loving little girl and God bless you.*'

A week later, he wrote, '*I'm quite settling down to bachelor life again, my sweetheart, tho I can't say I like it! I seem to miss you more every day, and it's a lonely home without my little girl to welcome me.*' Similarly, the following week he wrote: '*All my heart's love to you my own precious wife. Take great care of yourself and my little sons, and have a happy time. I'm too busy to be unhappy, but I long for you all the time and the house feels very lonely without my happy little family. God bless you. Give my little boys a kiss from their daddy. Bless them.*'

Arthur wrote to Euphemia in a similar loving way throughout 1915. He never ceased to miss her: '*I've got your photo on the mantelpiece beside me and shall kiss you goodnight before I get into bed. Goodnight, my best beloved. It's a cold night, and you'd want me to snuggle up close to you to get you warm and comfy, and I, how I'd love to be able to do so now, at once!*' He continued: '*Goodbye for this week my own sweet wife, another week of our separation gone, thank goodness. It's a rotten life out here without you,*' *darling, and all the time I want you. God bless you and keep you safe, and my little sons. I love you and them.'*

Money had been ordered to remain in India with his brigade for the course of the war, in case troops were needed to quell any uprisings or rebellions. As news reached him from the Western Front and the Dardanelles, he occasionally sounds frustrated in his letters not only to be away from his family, but also to be out of the action and unable to progress any further within the army. By June 1915, he seemed resigned to spending the war in India, and wrote to his wife asking her to join him. Euphemia sailed out to India in October, leaving the boys at home in England. The couple had only been re-united for two months, however, before their lives were turned upside down: in December 1915 Arthur was sent on active service and sailed for Mesopotamia.

Euphemia again returned to her family in Britain. Arthur served in the Middle and Near East until the end of the war, still writing regularly and affectionately to his wife, and was promoted to Chief Administrator of Palestine in 1918. He and Euphemia had a third son, James, in 1918, and a daughter Rosemary in 1922. He retired in 1920, as Major-General Sir A. W. Money, KCB, KBE, and CSI.

The most touching letter in the entire collection dates from December 1915, written at sea as Arthur sailed to Mesopotamia. Sailing away from India and towards the fierce fighting on the Mesopotamian front, anxious and apprehensive about the future, he wrote Euphemia a letter to be opened in the event of his death in service. This must have been a most precious letter to

Arthur Money (far left) in Baghdad in 1917.

Euphemia although thankfully, unlike many First World War widows, she never had to read it in the circumstances her devoted husband had intended.

On the envelope was written: '*To be kept by Alwyn Parker and handed over in accordance with the instructions contained in letter of 22/12/15 – should necessity arise – to Mrs A. W. Money. A.W.M. 22/12/15.*'

'S.S. Dumra 23/12/15

What shall I say to you, my sweet Beloved wife, for when, and if, you get this letter, I shall no longer be with you?

You have given me the happiest years of my life, Darling; and if I am not to have the final happiness of being at Home with you, and of seeing the little sons grow up, well, I have had more good fortune than falls to the lot of most men – far more than I deserve – and I thank God for it, and for the little sons and most of all for you, my best beloved.

You have been the sweetest and most loving wife, and may be happy in the thought of all the love and happiness you have brought into my life. I know you will be a wise and loving little mother to our sons; and I pray that they may grow up to be a blessing to you.

I wouldn't have you grieve for me too much, Darling; and I wouldn't have you – on my account – not marry again someday. You are young, and you will be lonely when the little sons grow up and go to school. I know they will be your first thought; and that, if you do marry again, it will be not only a man you can love and respect, but one who will be a good and loving father to the sons, as I would have tried to be ...

...You must talk to little David about his daddy; and tell him how dearly he loved his little sonny boy, and how he wants him to be a good and loving son to his mummy, and to always put the thought of her before everything else. My last thought will be of you, my Darling; and my last prayer will be in the words you wrote in my bible – that God will defend my Beloved and our little sons, keep them in body and soul, and grant that they and I may be bound together by the unseen chain of this love, by the communion of His Spirit, and by the Holy fellowship of His Saints; and that we may finally be together in his heavenly Kingdom.

God bless and keep you, my sweet and Beloved wife.'

RICHARD AND ETHELLE YEOMAN

Richard Harding Yeoman, a 28-year-old farmer, enlisted in the army on 11 September 1914. He was commissioned a second lieutenant from the 12th Gloucestershire Regiment exactly a year later. By then he was married, having wed Ethelle May Marshall in a Bristol register office the previous June. After recovering from an accident when his motorcycle collided with a milk cart, Richard was posted overseas. His destination would be Salonika in Greece where the British and French, having attempted to open a new front against Germany and the other Central Powers, were being held by the Bulgarians. As Richard sailed to join the 7th Battalion of the Wiltshire Regiment, Ethelle wrote him a lengthy letter in seventeen instalments between 28 September and 20 October 1916; she could not post it until she heard from him where he had gone. At the time

Ethelle was living with her parents-in-law at the Beeches, Mere, Wiltshire. She was still recuperating from giving birth to her baby son John, born barely a month earlier.

Ethelle begins her letter by letting her husband know that she has received a letter he wrote to her from the dock, just before embarkation.

'My very own,

It was nice of you to write again from Pembroke Dock. I am quite glad it was such a wet day! It was just the same here. A regular soaker. I am beginning a sort of diary of passing events, as I did when you went to Canada. I wonder when it will get posted – and where it will have to go. You will be wanting a letter by the time this arrives.'

She writes in an affectionate, lively, matter of fact way. Her letter is full of home news, and chronicles the everyday lives of the family; she writes about their friends and neighbours, about the local pig and horse sales, and even about a Zeppelin raid nearby. She keeps her letter straightforward and simple, making no mention of the difficulty of bringing up the baby in her husband's absence, and giving only the briefest hints of her inevitable anxiety at his safety: '*I can only trust that all will be well with you . . . As you may imagine you're in my thoughts many times.*'

The letter is couched firmly in the present, with little mention of the past, and none of the unknown future. Most often, she writes about John. Her letters are full of love for the baby, wonder at his development, and regret that Richard is missing it all. She describes the baby's morning visit to his grandfather,

Richard Yeoman (standing, centre) newly joined up in September, 1914.

her father-in-law, in the breakfast room: '*he* [the baby John] *gazes with wondering eyes at the cigarette smoke and is always greatly impressed with the glasses. Mr Yeoman usually greets him with "Well old man" and John grins all over his face – it really is funny to see him – he begins to regularly run this show.*'

The most moving aspect of the letter, however, is the way Ethelle does her best to maintain a relationship between the growing baby and his absent father. She writes that she will send her husband a lock of John's hair, as soon as it has grown long enough. She relates how often their acquaintance comments on John's obvious resemblance to his father. She describes the miraculous moment his first tooth comes through when he is only nine weeks old, a family record: '*Isn't he a precious infant?*'

She also describes the baby's reaction to Richard's photograph: '*John has been such a darling today – laughing all over his face at everyone. I always wish you could see him – it is so funny, each morning when I first pick him up he gazes at the large photograph of you above my bed and breaks into a big grin – he gets such a monster.'*

When Ethelle finally closes her letter ready for the post, a full four weeks after beginning it, she sends her husband a big kiss from the baby, alongside her own love: '*Shall write again very soon – am longing to know that this reached you. Write when you can darling and do take care of yourself. John sends a big kiss to his Daddy. You shall have more photographs next week. My very best and fondest love – Ever your loving wife, Ethelle.'*

Ironically, having taken Ethelle so long to complete the letter, it took even longer for it to reach her husband. No fewer than fifteen postal strikes on the envelope – the last of them dated 15 December 1916 – and the exasperated annotation 'Again not 2nd KSLI' (the letter had been addressed to Yeoman as attached to the King's Shropshire Light Infantry) suggest that he would have been lucky to have received his wife's news before Christmas.

SIDNEY EDWARDS AND
KIDDIE GOODALL

Gunner Sidney Ernest Edwards enlisted in the army on 9 September 1914 and served with the 20th Battery, the 1st/7th London Brigade of the Royal Field Artillery. He arrived in France on 18 March 1915 and, beginning in May, wrote one hundred and fifty letters to his sweetheart Miss Emma May Goodall, whom he called Kiddie. He wrote constantly about how much he looked forward to returning to her, and how much her letters meant to him: '*I hope you won't think I am greedy for letters, but you know it is very nice to hear from you.*'

By July, both Sid and Kiddie were feeling the strain of their separation. Sid's letters are painfully frank about how much he missed her, but he also wrote that thinking of her helped him through life at the front. '*My dearest Kiddie, I know it must seem a long time since I left England, but you are not to worry whatever you do, because I shall look after myself. I have got you to think of all the time, and that bucks me up a lot . . .*'

Sid wrote whenever he could to assure Kiddie that he was alive and well, but there were inevitably times when it was harder to write than others. There is a great contrast between the long, affectionate and humorous letters he was able to write when he had the time, and the loving but brief missives he sent when he was in action. '*Just a short letter to let you know that I am quite well, and that we have gone into action again, or at least our gun has and I have gone up with it as clerk, and my word, we shan't be sorry to get out again, for it's too warm for my liking, I don't mean the weather, I mean shells.*'

By August 1915, Sid was longing to see Kiddie, but any prospect of leave was still a long way off:

'*Well darling, how are you getting on, I should love to see you, I only wish I could get leave for a little while, but I am afraid I can't, and I am afraid it will be a long time before I see your sweet self again . . . I feel it enough, goodness knows, and you must feel it twice as much . . . you may be quite sure you are always in my thoughts and that I am quite true to you . . . and always shall be as long as I live.*'

By this time Sid had also had some pretty horrific experiences, which he felt unable to tell Kiddie about in his letters: '*Some of the scenery out here is very beautiful and I should like you to see it, because I know you would enjoy it, but then again, there are things out here which it would almost be impossible for you to see, you would never forget them as long as you lived. I will tell you all about everything when I get home, I know I shall never forget some of the things I have seen.'*

By October 1915, Sid's battery had endured months of fighting. He wrote to Kiddie about the strain of his periods at the front line: '*My dear Kiddie, do you know, we are all feeling better now we have had a rest, for I can tell you there is nothing on this earth that can play the devil so much with a fellow's nerves, as action. It is very trying, but you don't want to hear about our troubles, we are quite happy, at least I am as happy as can be expected after not seeing you or ma for so long.'*

By the beginning of 1916, Sid was homesick and missing Kiddie more than ever. In his first letter of the year, written in early January, he confided: '*I think I have been feeling a bit homesick this evening, I don't feel as if I can do anything . . . I have been thinking of you all day today and wishing I was with you . . . I wish you could send me a few of your sweet kisses, real ones, I mean . . . I hope I shall be able to have some before very long.'*

Two days later he wrote asking her to send him a hair ribbon as a keepsake, and told her his New Year's Resolution: '*I am very pleased with your good resolution to write more often, darling. To tell you the truth, I haven't made any myself, as I am afraid they would all get broken sooner or later; but I will make this resolution, dearest, and that is to love you more than ever, if that is possible . . .'*

In April 1916, over a year since he left England, Sid came home on a week's leave. Shortly after his return to the front, Kiddie's sister Annie married her fiancé George. Sid's letters from this period are extremely moving, as he was clearly and painfully torn between feeling that George, who was also serving in the war, was doing wrong by his new wife, and his own evident desire to marry Kiddie immediately despite the difficult circumstances:

'Now, honestly speaking, do you really consider it fair that George should get married just before he is going away? I don't, I think it is rather selfish of him, I consider it his duty to wait until he comes home again. I can guess that the joys of being married must be very, very nice, but surely he can wait a little while. I do not think it is at all fair to Annie. I am fond of Annie because she is your sister, darling, and the way I look at it is this: should anything happen to George, it will affect her ten times worse, and be so much harder for her. But anyhow darling it is not my business, so I shall wish them the very very best of luck ... Do you wish that we were married ...? I am sure I did when I was home. However love, everything comes to those who wait ...'

A letter from a few weeks later in May 1916 suggests that their relationship had intensified after his leave. It now seemed settled that they would marry on Sid's return at the end of the war. At the end of May, Kiddie turned twenty. Sid, who came from a farming family, sent her a lovely flirty letter on her birthday in which he imagines the pair of them living on a farm of their own:

'How would you like to have a farm my dear? I bet you wouldn't half get into a mess, and those little shoes of yours and your nice silk stockings would get all muddy, and then I suppose I could have the

pleasure of brushing them. I should like to be brushing a nice pair
of your silk stockings now, instead of trying to write letters, and of
course I don't mean empty ones. I believe I can see you blushing most
awfully when you read this, but you must forgive me . . . I know you
will, won't you?'

Sid had no more leave for the rest of the year, which must
have dragged terribly for the young couple. He had been transferred to C Battery of the 235th Brigade Royal Field Artillery
in November 1916, and in February 1917 he was promoted
to Bombardier. Their continuing separation did nothing to
dampen their ardour, however. In fact it seems to have done
quite the opposite. In May 1917, a year after broaching his feelings on the inadvisability of Kiddie's sister marrying a serving
soldier, Sid's emotions had got the better of him: '. . . *we*
shall have to have a glorious time when I do come home, in fact
I really think we ought to be married, even if we had to rush off
to a registry office, and then dash off the rest of my leave for a hon-
eymoon, that would be most enjoyable wouldn't it darling, just
think of it.'

   In a letter a few days later to celebrate her twenty-first birthday Sid wrote that since she was now a grown woman, perhaps
he should no longer call her Kiddie but should start to call her
May instead. He was expecting his next leave: he warned her
that he might not get much notice, and perhaps would surprise
her by arriving late at night unannounced.

'. . . *I am looking forward to seeing you more than anything else,*
and I should love to see you dressed all in white (and not much of

it). I believe that's how all young ladies have to dress nowadays, don't they, the less they wear the better it is. Anyway, I love white, you know the stuff I mean, very thin stuff with a lot of lace attached to it ... when I come on leave I shall probably roll home at an awkward time, probably at night, or anyhow, very late, so if you see me suddenly pulling you out of bed to kiss me, don't be a bit surprised, because that is exactly what I shall do if I get the chance. I know you wouldn't mind ...

Anyhow we have got all this to look forward to, so cheer up my own pet, I shall see you soon, with all my best kisses, big ones, and all my love for your dear little self, from

Your intended, Sidney xxxxxxxxxxxxxxxxxxxxxxxxxxx '

The museum also holds a few letters from Kiddie to Sid. They are undated, but easy to link to this period of their relationship, as they match the content of Sid's letters very closely. Kiddie wrote that she preferred he carry on calling her Kiddie rather than May. She was waiting desperately for Sid to come home on leave: ' ...*I had looked all the week for the post-man and began to wonder what was the matter ... I do hope you will soon be home. I only wish you could tell me when, but I would be quite satisfied if I knew if it would only be a few days and not weeks. This weather it makes me very miserable, or something does, I don't know if it is looking for you or what it is ... So good-bye dear with all my love to you. Longing for you ...*'

Tragically, just as the couple were so keenly awaiting his next period of leave in order to marry, Sid was killed on 14 June 1917, aged twenty-two. He wrote and posted a letter to Kiddie on the very day he died and had another ready to send among his belongings. This was forwarded to Kiddie in the letter sent from Sid's unit informing her of his death. In it, irony of ironies, he wrote how he had only recently narrowly escaped death.

'I hope I haven't kept you waiting too long for a letter ... We have had rather an eventful time just lately and I have had very little time to write. We had a shell drop in amongst our horses, and we all had an extraordinary escape, for we were all within ten yards of it. Two horses were blown to pieces, and several others were killed, or rather, hit so badly they had to be shot. My word, didn't we hurry and get those horses out of the lines. I should think we did it in record time. Well my dear how are you all at home, I hope you are all quite well and happy, we are happy enough ...'

PETER ROBINSON AND
DORRIE HARRIS

The British war effort in the First World War was backed by its world-wide empire. At Gallipoli in 1915 the British fought alongside Indian, Australian and New Zealand troops. The same year, during the Second Battle of Ypres, the Canadians won great renown by resisting the German offensive, notwithstanding their opponents' first use of poison gas. Then, in 1916, South African troops were committed to the Western Front in France. Among their ranks was 28-year-old Acting Bombardier Harry Robinson of the 71st Siege Battery, South African Heavy Artillery. Like many men of the dominions who answered the call of the mother country, Robinson – originally a sailor – was British-born, only emigrating to South Africa in the years immediately before the outbreak of war. His parents still lived in Blackheath, in south-east London.

Colonial troops serving in Europe thousands of miles from home were, for that reason, sometimes befriended by British women, often simply as pen-friends. Harry Robinson – who preferred to be called Peter – was taken up by one such girl, Enid Stanford, while training in England early in 1916. Enid knew just the person for Peter and effected an introduction to her friend Dorothy Harris, the twenty-year-old daughter of a prosperous farmer in Aston Abbotts, near Aylesbury. Peter visited in February and was immediately taken with 'Dorrie'. Thereafter he wrote to her once or twice a week. By the time of his fourth letter Dorrie was his 'petite demoiselle'. Peter became even more flirtatious in his eighth letter of 19 March 1916. There were rumours that his battery was about to leave for the front in France. He had to explain how he felt.

'Dorrie, there are so many things I wish to do before we go. Things are so different from peace-time when one can take one's time and not be importunate. I almost blush when I try to imagine what you think of me for turning up so often and being so bold. If I am given time I am a very polite, slow-stepping individual. I can assure you that in peace-time if I had seen you every day for a month it would still be a case of Miss Harris and Mr Robinson and not for another six months would I have dared to give you even a 9-carat gold cap badge. But needs must when the devil drives ...

... Perhaps you will sympathize with me if you can imagine yourself going away from everyone and everything perhaps for ever. I am quite harmless really, although I do like to pretend I am a bit

of a devil. But I am annoyed at the prospect of having to go away so soon.'

Although we only have, in the main, one side of the correspondence, it is clear that Dorothy was initially not unreceptive to Peter's boldness, prompting him to reply: '... *Thank you ever so much for your sweet, very Dorrie-like letter. But you must not tell me I am nice because people tell me I know that too well already. There you have it – I am conceited! I haven't seen you cross yet – I must make you cross with me just to see.'*

Unfortunately, it was not long before he succeeded. By 28 March, he had thrown off all restraint:

'... *Love never dies a natural death, but it may be killed – by starvation or by cruelty. That's the only way it ends, I'm certain. You, I already know from happy experience, will not be cruel to my tender flame and somehow I do not think that it will expire for lack of fuel. I don't mean to say that you will encourage it directly – it has only to think of you to shoot up into quite a dangerous blaze ...*

I was glad to get into my bed last night – terribly tired. Yesterday was a tiring day for me – anxiety fatigues me and so does the exercise of self-control. You will not understand me easily unless you have yourself had going on inside you a fierce struggle between inclination and right-doing. May I try to illustrate my meaning? Imagine a hungry child of the streets being made to stand in a restaurant without being allowed to eat. Imagine yourself in hell gazing hopelessly through the gates of heaven. Imagine Sisyphus with his eternal thirst as he stood up to his chin in the lake of clear water without being able to bow his head to drink. Imagine the

Peter Robinson (middle row, far right) with his comrades from
the 71st Siege Battery of the South African Heavy Artillery.

*Ancient Mariner when he saw water everywhere but not a drop to
drink. Imagine the condemned of the French Revolution when per-
mitted to say their last farewells to wives, sweet-hearts and children
through iron bars without touching them. Then you may be able to
imagine the nature of my feelings as I speak to and look on you . . .*

*This is the first time I have written to you without weighing my
words . . . Oh, I am glad I met you and I will ever try to be a source
of pleasure to you and never cause you to regret for a moment that
you have been kind to me. If you have not found it out already you
one day will find that most men abuse a woman's kindness, but I
don't think I do so . . . As I think of you I shall learn to love you
more. I am so very happy you do not mind me telling you I love you.
It is terrible to have to keep it to oneself.'*

This declaration of love might have, by itself, been enough to give a sensible woman like Dorothy pause for thought. However, Peter then wrote a second letter which proved altogether too much. Only in a few instances do we know how she reacted to his high-flown rhetoric, but we do on this occasion because she drafted her response first.

'Peter

I am so angry that I don't know how to write to you. I received both your letters this morning. I have it, on your own authority, that you, being a gentleman, would never abuse a girl's kindness, then you write and dare to suggest that I should envy your future wife and covet that honour myself! If that is not abusing my kindness, may I ask you what you consider would be? Because I allowed you to write pretty things to me (thinking it pleased you and did me no harm) is no reason for you to suppose that I'm in love with you. Your letter may of course be intended as a joke but if it is so it's in the worst possible taste, and even though I've known you for such a very short time I didn't expect it of you. If you still care to come down for the weekend after the following one I shall be as pleased as the others to see you, provided that you remember you have only seen me three times and apparently know me hardly at all . . .'

Peter was so mortified by Dorothy's reaction to his letters that he could not wait ten days to justify himself. He saw her that very weekend; at which point it seems that she told him plainly she did not feel about him as he did about her, but that she nonetheless valued him as a friend. Writing on 4 April to 'My Lady of Compassion', he felt reassured:

'I was very deeply touched that you came back to have another look at me ... Sunday was a lovely day for me, but yesterday was heaven. I cannot remember ever before being quite so contentedly happy. You were so sweetly gracious to me that I could not keep in my mind how horrible I had felt on Saturday ...

Lest you should think me a coward I read the angry letter last night. It made me squirm terribly, not on account of what you thought of me but on account of what you seemed to think I thought of you. I don't think my chastisement has done me any harm and I am very glad that I never had a thought which deserved it. If I had had such ideas of you as you imagined I had I don't know what I should do.

I shall burn the letter now and will you please burn that of mine which disappointed you?'

Robinson went to France at the end of April. His letters to Dorothy were now more decorous and routine. He took part in the Battle of the Somme, writing on 8 July: '*We have been warring very busily lately (since 1 July) and are still at it.*' On 25 July he described a reconnaissance in no man's land to observe the effect of fire at Pozieres. But his next spell of ten days' leave in England in January 1917, when he saw Dorothy once more, reawakened all his old feelings for her:

'I have just gazed into the fire and meditated for about half-an-hour. It is all very wonderful – to me, perhaps only silly to you. So wonderful

that I should see the good in you when I first met you; so wonderful that in the long months away from you the emotion which I at once assumed to be love should deepen instead of gradually fading away; so wonderful that I can feel so deeply and (I believe) so truly.

You have worked such wonderful changes in me. Before I met you I feared death but little and had not enough courage to dispel even that little fear. Now I fear death which entails parting from you for a long, long time, but now I have courage to face it and worse. And for the first time in my life I am frightened of a woman, the fear we all entertain of the unknown – for there is so much of you I don't know. I feel that you do not believe all of my serious expressions, and I do not know why that is . . . I only wish I could make you feel, for then you would believe me. As it is you seem to me to be quite cold and passionless and unable to understand. With all the wealth of sympathy you have extended to me in my troubles, great and small, I have found no grain of sympathy for my greatest trouble – my loving you. All this must sound utter rubbish to you unless you understand. You must think me mad to need sympathy for the thing which I have told you has done me more good than any other influences I have ever encountered. There are only two points on which I need sympathy – firstly, you don't love me; secondly, in a mad fit of patriotism I threw my prospects away in order to bear my part in this war and consequently for years am unlikely to be able to offer any woman more than just myself . . .

So you see what mental torture love must cause me. Such torture that duty, being the equivalent in this vile war to glory, would be doing me a kindness if its pathway led me to its proverbial end – the grave.

Well, dear Dorrie, circumstances I have explained prevent me trying to make you love me, but I go back to France to try my hardest, wherever the path may lead, to make you proud of me.

And that reminds me that I am enclosing with this a copy of a little piece of writing which is my proudest possession (I have not many other things to be proud of). Only the General who wrote it, the man who despatched it, my own Commanding Officer and myself have seen it, and I wish no one else except you to see it. I want you to have it in case Fritz does for me, for I have dedicated the deeds to you, their origin.

Good-bye,

Peter'

The medal citation he enclosed read as follows:

'Military Medal

No: 409 Acting Bombardier H. E .B. Robinson, 71st Siege Battery, South African Heavy Artillery.

For marked gallantry on two occasions in which he accompanied his Commanding Officer on daring reconnaissances under heavy shell-fire some hundreds of yards in front of our trenches in the face of the enemy's machine-guns and snipers. It was greatly to this Non-Commissioned Officer's coolness, judgement, loyal support and valuable assistance that his Commanding Officer was enabled to bring back information of the first importance to the Corps Commander.

On previous and subsequent occasions Bdr. Robinson has carried out dangerous reconnaissances, and observed for his battery, under conditions of great personal danger, with ability and bravery.'

Once back in France, Robinson's prose, always purple, became quite metaphysical. He wrote to Dorothy in one of two letters dated 27 February 1917:

'Do you think it probable that this war was started just so I should meet you? Extravagant, eh? Without it I should not know you. But this war is a high price for my soul, I'll bet I get billed. But I'll pay up. I am paying, goodness knows . . . I am beat to know what good my suffering does to God. For all the good it must do him he might as well give up the system of letting me hire a soul, and give me one outright with you and goodwill thrown in. I'd be good to you, dear, for the sake of the soul.

It's no good, old girl – you won't be able to read between the lines of my thoughts written as they are thought. You might generalize, that's all. If I put the last page into English it would read dully to me – at present it reads dully to you. All things lose by translation from their natural medium. If persons could read my thoughts some of those persons would, I really believe, love me.

It is a nuisance that the mind of each of us is a foreign language to all others – though there may be a key: perhaps with half-closed eyes and the soul in me now I might emit a jumbled murmuring that would be crystal clear to a love-tuned ear lying close to my lips. I think they are thoughts a woman would be proud to hear – perhaps – from, well from anyone. But I don't know. I never will know. But the war is going on and I shan't be able to do my part in it if I don't sleep and I have written a love-letter and meant to give up the habit and you won't recognize it as a love-letter, yet I must spoil things by telling you it's one, and make you think me

mad by saying it's the truest one I've ever written. But if you say
I'm nice in spite of my idiocy I'll be happy – though more idiotic
than ever.

   After all – it's only Peter'

Fate though was destined to play a cruel trick on Robinson.
Unrequited love is bad enough without being loved by someone
else you cannot love in return. Peter had cause to regret helping
a French girl behind the lines carry her produce to market, as he
explained to Dorothy on 23 September 1917:

'Cecile is getting beyond a joke – three letters from her in five
days. And what tears, what prayers, what protestations. I "must
spend my next leave there"; she "wants nothing from me, no
promises, no weddings, only a little corner in my heart". What
the deuce do I do next? She insists that I love her because I was
kind and "gentil". I was only polite – not so polite as I have been
to you; and you don't love me. I thought she would have got over
it by now. But it's early yet. What would you do? I cannot help
feeling that I am to blame, though it's not my fault if the child
is silly enough to think me worth all this waste of sentiment and
romance.'

At the beginning of December 1917 Peter was wounded and
sent back to England. Despite his best efforts to return to France
he was not allowed to do so and spent the remainder of the war
in Britain. It was some consolation that he could spend more
time with Dorothy. Staying with her in Buckinghamshire in
April 1918 was a highlight:

'I did not thank you for letting me sleep in your little room during the week-end. I am not quite certain of the way in which you regard such matters, but with me I could not so much as look inside your room unless you asked me to. To me there is something about your room which, just because it is yours, awes me somewhat. In the last few years I have slept in many queer places, among them a battered church. When I entered that church and dumped my filthy body and kit in it I saw no presence in it other than my comrades but I could feel awe and that feeling compelled me to make a silent apology to the Owner of the House! I went to sleep feeling very protected and contented. Silly sentimentality, perhaps, but I feel just the same in your little house ... Thank you very much. But perhaps you think that it is nothing you have done for me. My wife shall always have her own room – not our room – which to enter I shall ask permission, and therein worship her. She will not easily understand me unless she be a good woman – as what else could my wife be? – for one moment I will be kneeling at her feet and showing her the spots and patches on my soul and the next moment I will be chasing her along the passage in her pyjamas with the bristly end of a back-scrubber. She will have to be both my God and my pal. Do you see?'

The war was coming to an end and although Peter would continue to write to Dorothy until 1926, there was something almost valedictory in the words that he wrote to her on 17 September 1918: *'Nothing can be far wrong in a world which enables me to dream of your arms and lips: yet this same good world allows me no feel of them – thank God. When the time comes that you resign yourself to big arms, strong arms, you will be able to*

Portez-lui mes vœux.
I send my greetings to you.
Лучшія пожеланія.

2732

Two of the postcards sent by Andrew Thorne to his daughter Deeney. On the first he wrote: 'I think that this little girl must surely catch the "flu" as her costume is not very warm.'

THE NEW LOVE

Son nouvel amour

Reginald Stephens sent this German Christmas card, captured at Neuve Chapelle in March 1915, to his daughter, remarking: 'I think it is rather like you!'

The much-travelled letter sent by Ethelle to Richard Yeoman, with its multiple redirections and exasperated note: 'again, Not 2nd KSLI'.

The hillside above Dover where Alan McPeake met Eileen Linn. Painted by Alan as the view from my tent'.

Cheer up, the first **7** years will be the worst.

The humorous card sent by May Utton to her husband Freddie in May 1917. At the top is her pencil note, now very faint, which reads: 'I'm fed up with the first three, let alone 7'.

Enormous numbers of hand-embroidered postcards were produced in France and Belgium for soldiers to send home. Many of the cards sent by Holland Chrismas to his sweetheart Ada Manley were of this type.

Sweetheart brooches, small jewelled representations of regimental or unit badges, were given by serving officers to their wives and girlfriends. This one, with the badge of 11th King Edward's Own Lancers and his photograph on the reverse, was given by Major (later General Sir) Alan Fleming Hartley to his wife Philippa after he returned to France from leave (hence the dates).

Remember Me
When around thee dying
Your comrades are lying
Oh, then remember me
And at night when gazing
On the gay hearth blazing
Oh still remember me.

Cards such as this with 'Remember me' verses were produced both for soldiers to send to their loved ones and, as shown here, for women at home to send to their men at the front.

I have something to say to you it is?

20/9/15

I wonder if I dare

With Best Wishes & Fond Recollections
of Lucy.
                    Gunner W. Lyman. R.F.A.

Wounded soldiers not unnaturally became attached to those who
tended them and left sentimental messages and drawings in their
nurses' autograph books, like these from Gunner Lyman (above)
and Private Winter (below).

Not in the Prescription

"*To You*"

The soldier and his sweetheart became a popular subject for artists during and immediately after the First World War. The top illustration of a fashionable flapper and her soldier writing to her from the trenches is an advertisement for De Reszke cigarettes. The painting by Richard Caton Woodville is titled 'We saw you going, but we knew you would come back' and depicts the entry of the British 5th Lancers into Mons on Armistice Day, 11 November, 1918.

think kindly and without shame of the ass Peter who loved you and whose arms you never knew.'

Perhaps he might even have sensed that a rival was about to appear on the scene. On 26 November 1918 Dorothy received a letter from Lieutenant Charles Meredith of the Royal Air Force:

'Dear Miss Harris,

Some time ago, Enid Stanford wrote and sent me your address asking me to call and see you as an old friend of hers.

In a later letter she said you would be pleased to see me. This is very kind of you and I must apologize for not having written before.

Supposing I was to fly up to your place from here, is there any convenient field, in which I could land, near by . . .?'

And so it started again. Within a short time Meredith was hopelessly in love with 'Fluffy'. He proposed and was rejected.

Dorothy never married.

LEE ELLIS AND PEGGY

'Could have yelled with joy on receiving 2 letters from you yesterday evening, only I was in the orderly room where such things aren't done. Thanks most fearfully for them.'

Henry Lee Ellis wrote one hundred and fifty-eight letters to his girlfriend Peggy during the course of the First World War, from early 1916 until spring 1918. During that two-year period he saw Peggy four times on brief periods of leave.

Lee, as he called himself, served in France, first as a lieutenant with the 11th Sherwood Foresters and later with the 16th Labour Battalion of the Yorkshire Regiment. He had an incredible variety of duties, from collecting stores and running a cinema for the troops to managing teams of German prisoners of war building roads and overseeing the loading and unloading of supplies at a dock. His letters to Peggy, which he is worried she will find boring due to his lack of news, are actually full of detail and reveal the unpleasant realities of First World War army life with incredible clarity: wasps in his tent, bugs in his bedding, the misery of the cold, the wet, and the mud, the noise of the guns, and the awfulness of the shells. He mentions his late nights and early starts and never having enough sleep, together with the sheer joy of an occasional bed with sheets after months of sleeping on the floor.

Like most soldiers, however, Lee was not one to complain about his position, and despite the difficulties of the campaign his letters are written with much humour and a genuinely positive outlook.

'My dear Peggy

Thanks ever so much for your letter. I only wish I had half as much to tell you but things go on here very much the same day after day with a few unpleasant varieties. We have had one of them to-day. They threw some of their shells unpleasantly close here; of course we are within easy range of their guns; but it wasn't nice of them was it? It was quite big stuff too, sounded something like a tired aeroplane coming over. Beastly sound . . .

I wish I was helping you to wind that wool. Great fun it would be. At present I am sitting in my very cold room, cold because the windows are all gone and are only boarded up in places, and writing this letter on my knees. My feet are like blocks of ice too. So I am in a pretty bad way you see, I.D.T. [I don't think]. Must stop now, go and get some tea and then off to the cinema show. Quite

a good programme this week. Wouldn't you like to come and see it?
Do write again soon.
    Best love
    Yours affectionately
    Lee'

Alongside the monotony of his various duties, Lee wrote about the films, plays, concerts, and even opera performances he was sometimes able to attend in his free time. He tells her funny stories about the horses he works with, who find the icy conditions troublesome ('*my whole attention was spent keeping my horse on her feet. She tried to sit down on several occasions*'), and are extremely puzzled on meeting a tank. He tells her how, when he administered a quantity of rum to a horse suffering from colic, it promptly spat the liquid back in his face, leaving him reeking of spirits.

In his letters he often characteristically makes light of his situation; and yet beneath the levity, the stark truth of the conditions he had to endure comes through. On 17 September 1917 he writes that he '*had just come down out of the trenches and it was very rough up there, especially coming down last night. However, we got through alright. At present I am at my transport lines and shall be employed with my Brigade Pack Company, taking rations, etc. up the lines. Expect it will be pretty lively work too, but hope it won't be as bad as it was last night . . . This is a very different sort of war to what it was 2 years ago.*'

On 24 December he writes Peggy a Christmas letter: '*Weird sort of Xmas Eve this. Snow on the ground, barbed wire compounds all round and tanks about 50 yards away . . . By Jove it was cold last night. I turned out at 3 a.m. to visit my guards and got absolutely frozen. My feet ... remained so till midday. Put the wind up me, I really thought they were frostbitten. Can hardly see to write this as the wretched stove is smoking. We are burning damp logs of wood and of course the smoke is fearfully painful. Don't be surprised if a large tear drop falls on this letter.*

... I expect you are having skating in London by now. This country would be very nice for toboganning only there are too many old shell holes and dugouts knocking about to make the pastime quite healthy. You would get up a beautiful speed and then come an awful smash in some place hidden by the snow.'

He was, however, careful to protect his sweetheart from much of the full horror of his experiences, warning her not to listen to stories and rumours back in England: '*Cheer up Peggy. People have no right to tell those sort of yarns at home. I could tell you some delightful stories of my last 4 months in the line, and of the things I saw and had to do, but I'm not going to.*' In spite of their long separation, he does his best to remain involved in Peggy's own life, regularly enquiring how her medical studies are going, wishing her luck in her exams and warning her not to work too hard.

Lee's favourite topic is the letters themselves; he talks about writing his and receiving hers. He is thrilled when one of her letters smells of her 'hairwash', and she evidently teases him that his smell of tobacco. He discusses how long her letters take to reach him, and which of his letters she has received. He often describes the difficulty of writing by candlelight with the paper balanced on his knee, and asks her to excuse the pencil, as his fountain pen will only work when he has a table to write on, which is not often.

He has other writing issues too: '*Someone is playing pieces from the "Bing Boys" and "Theodore and Co" [on the gramophone], one after the other, so it's rather difficult to write as my pen will try and go in time to the music . . . The finding of an envelope for this letter is going to be rather a problem. Every envelope I have discovered so far is stuck down fast with the damp. There are unfortunately two holes in my tent so it is not exactly dry there.*' The strongest theme of his letters, however, is the fact that it is her letters, together with the thought of seeing her again on leave, that support him and get him through: '*Goodbye for the present Peggy. Do write me very soon. That and my next leave are all I have to look forward to. (Sounds like suicide doesn't it.) Heaps of love, Lee.*'

Lee Ellis survived the war, and was joyfully reunited with his sweetheart. The last letter in the collection was written to her from Oxford, on Armistice Day, 11 November 1918. Back in England, among the celebrations, Lee was still finding writing conditions difficult: '*Oxford has gone absolutely mad. Expect the town will be in ruins tomorrow. Anyhow things will be pretty merry here this evening . . . PS. I have not been celebrating yet. My [erratic] writing is caused by writing in semi-darkness and on a very shaky table.*'

Holland and Ada Chrismas

The postcards sent by Private Holland 'Holly' Chrismas to his sweetheart back home in London, Miss Ada Manley, were chiefly sentimental, and include many embroidered silk postcards. The latter are especially vibrant, colourful and pretty examples of an art form manufactured in France and sent home in huge numbers by British troops on the Western Front during the First World War.

Embroidered silk postcards were first produced in France, Germany, Switzerland and Austria in the early part of the twentieth century, and continued to be made until 1945. Their heyday was the First World War period, however, when millions were produced, especially in France and Belgium. The greetings cards Holly sent to Ada nearly all belong to the 'Hearts and Flowers' category of postcards, but many other

Holland and Ada Chrismas with Eric, their baby son.

types were produced showing regimental or patriotic designs, some even incorporating photographs of French and British military leaders.

The postcards were hand-embroidered. It is likely that much of the embroidery was done by nuns around the invaded areas of Belgium and northern France, working together with refugees to support their income. The designs were embroidered on a roll of silk or organdie using coloured silk thread. Identical designs were worked on the same piece of cloth, before being separated, mounted on card and framed. Towards the end of the war, some parts of the embroidery on the designs would have been prepared by machine.

Holland Chrismas himself had enlisted in the British Army as a fourteen-year-old boy in 1904 and, until he was commissioned into the King's Shropshire Light Infantry in September 1917, served in the cavalry, first the 9th Lancers and then the 1st Royal Dragoons. Holland married Ada a month after his promotion, but it is apparent that the path of true love had not always run smooth. On 29 July 1916 Holland sent Ada a strikingly different postcard from his others, showing instead the execution of Nurse Edith Cavell, shot by the Germans in Belgium in 1915 for helping British soldiers escape captivity. On the reverse was the cryptic message: '*Dear A. Am still looking out for a letter. Feeling very uneasy. Much love Holl.*' What was the subliminal message of the choice of postcard: did Holland fear that, like Nurse Cavell, the love that Ada once bore him had been murdered?

Only when he wrote three months later in October, however, do we get an inkling of what had happened. Holland had

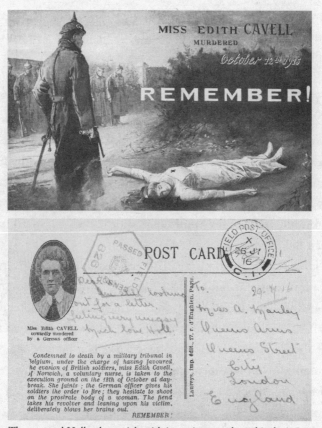

The postcard Holland sent Ada with its ominous and graphic depiction of the death of war heroine Nurse Edith Cavell.

been home on leave in July, and on a day out he and Ada had a terrible row: '*I know dear you did not enjoy that day, and what a beastly temper you got into going home. You did make me feel wild for a few moments.*' Evidently the rift had not been entirely healed by the time Holland returned to France; hence his anxiety. But fortunately love had not been murdered, and Holland was soon able to tease Ada once again, just like old times: '*Thank you dearest very much for the nice parcel, in which I found one of your handkerchiefs with "A" marked on it. [It] was with the Cake, will send it back later on, when I've washed it.*'

A son, Eric John Holland Chrismas, was born to the couple in May 1918, by which time Holly was a second lieutenant in the Machine Gun Corps. Holly remained in the army for another five years, resigning his commission in July 1923.

ARTHUR AND MAY NEILSON

When Sergeant Arthur Hunter Neilson first left for the Great War in October 1914 it was with the London Scottish, a Territorial Force regiment. No sooner had he landed in France than Neilson, a thirty-year-old produce merchant in civilian life, was shot through the left calf during the Battle of Messines. Evacuated back to London, eighteen days in hospital at Whitechapel saw him recover and he was rewarded with a commission in the Gordon Highlanders.

In the autumn of 1916, when he left for France again, Neilson was a lieutenant in the 7th Signal Corps, Royal Engineers, attached to the 7th Division. Warfare had changed rapidly in the intervening two years and effective battlefield communication was now a priority. The signal branch operated rapidly advancing telephone and wireless systems and had, as a result, grown exponentially.

Arthur Neilson in the uniform of the London Scottish.

To be parted again from his wife, May, and his young daughter Peggy, whom he called 'Tingy', was no doubt hard for Neilson. Arthur wrote from St Albans to May in Richmond-on-Thames on the eve of his departure for France. He had sent her a telegraph hoping to arrange a final meeting but to no avail, leaving him to say goodbye by letter:

'Sweetheart

I wired you this morn asking you to come here if possible this evening, but I suppose you were unable to get here. I cannot explain in this note the whys and wherefore of events. We are off to Paris in the morning, for to protect the lines. We leave Trafford at 9.25 for Southampton. I have watched every conveyance on the road for you, but none contained the one I wanted, so by this I must say "Au Revoir" for a few weeks. May the kind Providence watch over us both in the meantime. Keep a stout heart Little Girl and don't worry about me or about money, as I told you, you know where to write. I will send you my address as soon as I can ... God be with us till we meet again. Kiss Tingy for me and my everlasting love to you. Arthur'

Over the next three years Arthur wrote several letters to Tingy directly. The first was in October 1916, when she was finallly old enough to read a letter for herself. '*You have waited for a long long time for your own letter so here it is, all to yourself alone, and even mummy is not getting one today, she will tell you that she does not get one every day.*' The second was sent to mark her birthday a few weeks later, the third was sent in the summer of the following year, and the fourth again to mark her birthday and Christmas in late 1917.

7th Corps Signals

Dear little Sweetheart Tingy

You have waited for a long long time for your own letter so here it is, all to yourself alone, and even Mummy is not getting one today, she will tell you that she does not get one every day,

I am very busy now and have very little time to myself, I have to go all round the country, and be in six places at once, you might try doing that one day, it is quite easy when you have learnt it, but please dont try it too often or you will not be there when I come home

I see you must be doing quite well at school, you write quite nicely, you must be learning quite a lot of things now, all about 'everything! and reading by yourself.

You must take care of your self and not catch any nasty Colds

Well I have to finish now, and will write you again,

Many hugs and lots of love to you and Mummy   Good-night
                    Daddy

Arthur's first letter to Tingy, written in his beautiful copperplate hand.

The letters are jokey and light-hearted: '*I am very busy now and have very little time to myself. I have to go all round the country and be in six places at once. You might try doing that one day, it is quite easy when you have learnt it, but please don't try it too often or you will not be there when I come home.*' They are very affectionate, addressed to '*little Sweetheart Tingy*' and '*My Dearest Little Girl*', telling her not to catch colds, asking about her schoolwork, and teasing her for mixing up the words 'buy' and 'bye' in her letters to him.

He tells her about the birds and flowers he encounters even right at the front line: '*The fields out here look very nice and green with lots of buttercups and daisies, and ever so many dandylions* [sic], *even right up to where the fighting is going on . . . Just now I am in a wooden hut and the birds have built a nest, but there was a terrible accident, someone knocked it down and the poor little birds were in a terrible state, but we fixed it up they built it again and are using it now. I expect there will be some eggs soon.*'

In his last letter, Arthur wished his daughter a very happy birthday in his absence for a second time: '*Many happy returns of today and a very happy Xmas. With fondest love to you and Mummy. Your loving Daddy.*'

Thankfully, the Neilson family was one of the lucky ones. Arthur survived the war and, after service with the post-war British Army of Occupation in Germany, returned home to his wife and Tingy in November 1919.

TEDDY AND MOLLY MURPHY

In August 1916 Sergeant Edward 'Teddy' Murphy of Number 2 Company Army Service Corps, part of the 6th Divisional Train, was courting Molly Chewe of Portslade, Sussex. Discussion turned to getting a marriage licence but Teddy cautioned Molly to wait until he was either next on leave or the war had been won; there were still some who had hopes that the Battle of the Somme would lead to victory before the year's end. '*Well dearest, as regards the licence, don't pay any more until you hear from me as I am afraid it will be a long time before leave starts again. In fact I don't believe it does, but I shall have to wait and see; we want the war finished first if possible. I can assure you that I don't want another winter out here.*'

By December 1916, following a spell of leave, they were married and Teddy delighted in addressing Molly in his letters as

'My Own Darling Wife'. He enjoined Molly to be good: *'No flirtation now, eh! I am not been* [sic] *sarcastic. Never mind dear, I know you are my wife and will remain true to your dear Hubby.'*

The winter of 1916–17 was as hard as Teddy had feared it might be, but he bore up. He was a conscientious soldier and, being in supply, he felt personally responsible for ensuring that 'the boys' in the trenches got everything they needed. On 24 February 1917 he gave Molly his latest news and expressed his hopes for the future:

'The boys are out for a rest and of course it makes plenty of work for me besides a good march every day and by the time I reach my billet I am fatigued, but to-night I happened to get in early so I make it my first duty to catch tonight's post ... I sincerely hope to be by your bedside before the year is out and never more to be parted. My word shall I not stick to my good bed and indeed appreciate it; like me there will be thousands of others only waiting for the final ending and the sooner it comes the better for everybody.'

In June 1917 Teddy transferred to the quartermaster's stores of the 8th Battalion the Bedfordshire Regiment. He wrote to Molly the following month, looking forward once again to the end of the war but also expressing his concern that she try and keep clear of the German bombing of England. For civilians to be in danger as well as soldiers was a new phenomenon to which everyone had to get used:

'I am busy just now and will be for a few days, so you must expect a short letter; and our boys are going to have a rest in some quiet

country village. Well dear I am A1, and trust to keep so till the war is finished to enable us to have our good and full married pleasures which now seem so distant. Yes dear I am making good use of the bicycle, plenty of work and the machine makes it a pleasure, the lesson I have so often heard from you; yes dear the weather is simply great and I should love to have our arms in close especially you in your white costume and me in my navy blue suit. Ah, those are the times we [have] got to come. Oh yes leave is still going strong and I want it so as my turn will come all the quicker ... Enjoy your holiday at Eastbourne ... I don't want you to get into the danger zone as aeroplanes are very busy this fine weather ... and I don't want you to give those seaside young men the glad eye, eh what?'

Just because Teddy and Molly were not together in person did not mean that they could not bicker like any other married couple. On 28 August 1917 Teddy metaphorically wagged his finger at her:

'I was really upset over you as your letter never reached me for 11 days after postage as you did not copy my address correctly, you must not put 'Train' on, as I am staying now with the Stores like I was at Shoreham owing to new systems, so you will be careful in future won't you ... how many places your letter went to I do not know ... You also state about a parcel, well I have never seen it yet and if it was addressed the same as your letter I may never get it; still I have said enough about that ...'

Fortunately, Molly's parcel did arrive and Teddy, writing on 1 September, was ecstatic: *'Your dear letter and photo were waiting on my return and oh how pleased I feel, and even now while my pencil is working I am gazing on you with awestruck eyes waiting to put my arms around [you] and kiss your dear lips, you look charming and I must say rather saucy which I like ...'*

After a little verbal jousting about whose fault it was that Molly's letters had been misaddressed ('*Oh no dear I never put "Train" on my letters now'*, Ted protested), Molly got her chance to complain about Teddy when she reported that one of his letters had reached her unsealed. He defended himself against the imputation of carelessness: '*I am sorry my letter was not stuck down when it reached you but I can assure you that I am most careful in sticking my letters down ... it must have come unstuck in transit ...'*

In February 1918, after heavy losses in the previous two years of fighting, shortage of manpower in the British Expeditionary Force in France meant that a number of infantry battalions had to be disbanded, the 8th Bedfords among them. At first Teddy did not know where he would be sent, though Molly had her fears. She was anxious that he might end up working in too close proximity to members of the Women's Army Auxiliary Corps (WAAC). Raised in 1916 in order to release men from administrative tasks for the front line instead, the WAAC was before long beset by unfounded rumours of immorality. Teddy hastened to assure Molly that the WAAC girls were not his type: '*... oh no WAAC are on my job dear they are not so far up country as that ... there are quite a good number here on the station but I have nothing to do with them whatsoever, I think they are too brazen altogether.'*

WAACs sorting uniforms together with their male colleagues.

On 20 March Teddy reported to Molly that he had been posted to the 2nd Bedfords, but he had also applied for a commission as an officer and so might yet end up somewhere else. Little did he know that the following day the Germans would unleash a massive offensive, Operation Michael, which they hoped would win the war. While the attack was eventually stemmed, it would be at the cost of much territory and many lives. But what fate had befallen Teddy? Molly must have imagined terrible things when she received a letter, post-dated 1 April, from the 15th Convalescent Depot of the BEF. In fact, the reason for his presence there proved somewhat anti-climactic:

'My Own Darling Wife

I dare say you are anxiously waiting news of me. Well dearest you can see I am at a convalescent camp after going through 8 days of fighting. I got a slight back strain and could not stick the pain any longer so had to go sick to get it better. I expect to be here for a few weeks and all your previous letters I am enquiring about so that they find me. Well dearest it's a treat to be alive I can assure you but still the spirit is good amongst all the troops . . .

. . . I must bid you adieu with all my love and kisses for our future welfare.

From your ever loving Hubby
Ted

PS. It was impossible for me to write before and let you know anything, but now all is well.'

Teddy never got his commission but survived the war. For Molly that would have been enough.

William and Edith Harper

William Harper joined up and left for France in December 1916. He left behind his 'Dear Wifie' Edith and their two young sons William and Stanley. For the next two years, Harper's companions were the men of 6 Platoon, B Company 1st/4th Battalion of the Suffolk Regiment. He wrote to his wife regularly, complaining bitterly about his life with the British Expeditionary Force. He loathed the December weather, the snow, and the mud: '*I never knew what mud was until I came over here.*' His boots were always wet, his feet were always cold, he did not get enough food and often he did not get a change of clothes for weeks at a time. He slept packed into a tent with many other men, and they woke up each morning to find the inside of the tent and their blankets covered in frost. The water froze and they couldn't wash, and they all suffered terribly from lice.

After some initial training, Harper and his companions were issued with their front-line equipment, which they struggled to carry: '*viz steel helmet, and various other impediments; by the time we get loaded up, we shall hardly be able to stagger along.*' He found it hard to sleep with the noise from the guns and the shells, and on Christmas Eve 1916, as he lay packed in his tent '*like a sardine*', he remembered previous Midnight Masses at home with his family and thought, '*God grant that if I am spared, that I may never have to spend such another Xmas.*'

Letters and parcels from his wife were his only consolation. '*I shall be so glad to see your handwriting once more*', he wrote to her; and again, '*Your long letter was a god-send to me this afternoon and I have already read it through twice.*' When Edith sent him his first food parcel in January 1917, he wrote back, '*I have never enjoyed anything so much before*'. William found it hard to write to her, however, knowing that his letters would be censored, and as he pointed out, '*it is so difficult here to write all one feels; it is different when one can sit in the quiet in one's own room, but [not] here where comfort is absent and noise and interruptions are frequent, not to say anything of stone cold feet and squatting on the floor huddled up.*'

Edith must have been thrilled to receive letters from her husband when they contained such heartfelt statements as the one he sent in late January 1917: '*as I sat and thought of you, I did realize what a darling old wife you have been to me, and how thankful I ought to be for it ... I do so love you, and I know you realize my deep affection for you, I am constantly thinking of you and praying for your safety and for our speedy re-union, when I shall indeed show you how deeply I love and treasure you.'* William also missed his two young boys, and often sent them separate kisses at the bottom of his letters: '*I should love to be home now to see our dear little boys growing up and their quaint little ways.'*

William's time apart from his wife made him reassess their relationship, and gain a fresh understanding of the depth of their feelings and devotion for each other. '*I am always think-ing of you, my dear, and all the happy times we have spent together. We do love each other so very much don't we, and now our sepa-ration makes us realize this to the full. I wonder how long before we see each other again. Like you I feel quite hopeless at times, I go up and down like a thermometer, I do so long for the time when we shall once more be together again . . .'*

As 1917 progressed, William wrote to his wife of his constant trials: more mud, rain, colds, neuralgia, lack of food, and the incessant routine of life at the front; a few weeks in the trenches living in dugouts, a few weeks on fatigue work carrying heavy loads during the night hours, and the rare welcome rest billeted in French villages behind the lines. Meanwhile, at home, his wife had her troubles too. Unable to cope financially without her husband, she moved their young family into her mother's house and rented out their own home. Wiliam felt unable to help or advise: '*dear, as I have said before, it is for you to do what you like, as out here I have no brain left, and am only thankful at the end of each day to find myself alive.'*

William's letters often mention how sorry he is that she is feeling depressed, and that he understands how hard it must be for her waiting for his return and bringing up the boys alone.

He often wrote in great depth about the things that kept his own spirits down; he especially regretted the fact that he was '*missing Willie's baby days*'. However, he also wrote that the separation was strengthening their relationship, and how much they would appreciate each other once reunited: '*to be sure I shall love you umpteen times more than I ever did before*'.

As Harper approached his second winter on active service at the front, the tension and strain he was under became increasingly clear. '*Doesn't it all seem so hopeless and endless, this war,*' he complained. '*There seems no signs of any ending and how sick to death everyone is of the whole thing. It requires a great deal of patience to keep calm and hopeful: I am afraid that I have nearly reached the limit.*'

In a letter of October 1917 he wrote to Edith describing his dugout: '. . . *or rather it is more of a tunnel with timber supports and wire bunks along each side like a ship, it is quite dark inside day and night so we have to burn umpteen candles which we have at times a difficulty to buy at the canteens. It is very narrow and where I am, there has evidently been a shell drop on it and it has caved in the timber which is all cracked and the supports knocked out of place making it even narrower. Plenty of stinking water up our end, it gets so stifling and hot in the evening what with the tobacco smoke and the candles, I have bumped my head umpteen times on the beams.*' On Christmas Day he wrote and told her of his pitiful festive meal of stew and Christmas pudding.

In January 1918, having been away from his family for a year, William was granted leave and returned home for a brief but joyful visit. On his journey back to France he wrote to Edith:

'My own darling wifie, I can just imagine how glad you will be when the postman arrives with this, I only wish that I was the postman. What a lovely hug and kiss I would give you ... Sweetheart I do love you passionately, you cannot realize the depths of my love and devotion towards you, for I am unable to express it in words, as I am rather a quiet sort of boy. What a wrench it will be to leave here in the morning and feel myself being taken farther and farther away from you ... God bless and keep you and give you that patience and courage which I know you require now, for I do realize fully what a hard part you have to bear and how terribly you must now miss me. Kiss the dear little chappies for me.'

He wrote that while with her on leave he was *'yes – in Heaven'*. After the joy of seeing each other again, however, it was back to the grind of their days apart. Harper returned to the lice, shells and mud of the trenches while Edith coped alone with domestic emergencies such as Stanley's measles and young William's whooping cough.

Husband and wife wrote constantly throughout the spring and summer of 1918, until in the autumn, in October, Edith received a letter from William written from a hospital in France: *'Here I am old girl, installed in a Base Hospital. I got slightly wounded in the throat on Friday night.'* He had been wounded by a shell, and was evacuated back to Britain: *'I thought my head was going to be blown off, so I was lucky to get off as I did.'* He wrote again from a hospital in Oxford, his last letter to his wife before returning home to her, telling Edith about his experience:

'When I was wounded I had my steel hat on and ... had to walk that Friday night (in company with another chap in my platoon who was wounded by the same shell and our Captain who was also hit in the arm) such a long way, must have been a couple of miles to the nearest Aid post and Fritz was shelling all round us. It was an awful journey stumbling along through trenches etc. in the dark, but still we got there, that's the main thing. Then we were alright, they put me on a stretcher and soon we were away in a motor ambulance.'

He signed this final letter '*from your* devoted *hubbie*'. Painful and difficult as this time must have been for both of them, there is no doubt that his two years of war service only strengthened their love.

FREDDIE AND MAY UTTON

Couples separated by the First World War engaged in many different kinds of correspondence. Freddie Utton, a 24-year-old accountant's clerk from Balham in London, had enlisted in the Queen's Royal West Surrey Regiment on 30 November 1915 and married his wife May Cecilia 'Mayche' the following July. Throughout 1917 and 1918 they sent each other a series of light-hearted, comical postcards.

While her husband was serving with a depot company at the regiment's command depot in Tipperary, Ireland, in April 1917, May sent him a postcard showing a sexy girl lifting weights with the caption 'I'm also in training, to give you a good hug on your return.' On the back she cheekily wrote, '*How do you like my new photo, like me.*' A few months later she sent him a real photograph of herself, in which she does

May Utton.

indeed bear quite a striking resemblance to the girl on the postcard!

In May 1917 she sent him a postcard showing a small child dressed as a soldier with the caption 'Cheer up, the first 7 years will be the worst.' Across the top she has written '*I'm fed up with the first three, let alone 7!*' Such light-hearted and mischievous missives must have really helped Freddie keep his spirits up during his service, especially when he found himself posted to the Italian front with his regiment's second battalion following the victory of the Germans and their Austrian allies over Britain's ally Italy at Caporetto in October 1917.

I'M ALSO IN TRAINING,
TO GIVE YOU A GOOD HUG ON YOUR RETURN

The postcard about which May asked:
'How do you like my new photo …?'

Finally, months after the war had ended, May received a post-card from her husband from a rest camp at Faenza in July 1919 with the wonderful news that he was on his way home. In keeping with the breezy tone of their wartime correspondence he wrote: '*I have not written before owing to my being shifted about so much, but I do not think you will mind now I am actually on my way ... Cheerio till I see you in a few days' time.*'

WILLIAM AND NELLIE ADAMS

Sergeant William Stanley Adams was taken prisoner by the advancing Germans as he fought with the 1st Battalion of the Inniskilling Fusiliers (part of the 36th Ulster Division) on 22 March 1918, during the Battle of St Quentin, the first engagement of the Second Battle of the Somme. The fighting was so fierce during this period that three British divisions were effectively destroyed and had to be taken out of the order of battle to be rebuilt. Of them, Adams' Ulster division was the worst affected, losing 7,310 men, many of whom, like him, were taken captive.

Adams, who used his middle name, Stanley, had had a pretty colourful war record even before he was captured in 1918. His battalion took part in the Gallipoli landings in April 1915, where he was wounded and evacuated to Malta for medical treatment. He recovered and rejoined the battalion, which was then evacuated from the peninsula to Egypt in early 1916. He later wrote a memoir in which he remembered eating a Christmas pudding from a tin with the tip of his bayonet, alone in a forward sniping post in Gallipoli in December 1915.

Stanley transferred briefly to the 8th Royal Irish Hussars in 1916–17, and during this period he married Miss Nellie Colhoun in Londonderry in August 1916, with whom he went on to have a son, also called Stanley. He rejoined the Inniskilling Fusiliers in time to fall victim to the massive German spring offensive of 1918. As a prisoner of war, he was held in a series of camps: Langensalza, Cassel and then Werben, from which he managed to escape, only to be recaptured after several days on the run, whereupon he was transferred to Gardelegen.

In a letter sent to his mother in April 1918, Stanley gives lots of detail about his life as a prisoner of war at Langensalza: '*I am sure you will have heard the news from poor Nell about me by now . . . I am real well Mother and getting settled down to this life if I only had a parcel and some smokes. I have not had a cig now for 4 weeks . . . I know the girls will all subscribe a shilling or two and try and send me a bit of bread and tinned stuff such as syrup, jam, condensed milk, tea and sugar, black puddings, cheese and things like that to keep . . . We get 3 meals here every day, but not like what we were accustomed to . . . I can receive as many letters as I like but can only write 2 letters and a card a month . . . I lost everything. I have only a spoon and 2 handkerchiefs and a watch. I have a good clean bed here in a good Barrack hut, fires and all in it, 2 blankets and we get baths and clean clothes regular. We were*

William and Nellie Adams, shortly after their wedding.

vaccinated and inoculated 4 times so we are fairly all right from disease . . . Poor Nell won't be able to send me much from her money, I have no razor and not a scrap of soap. I have washed with clay for the last 4 weeks . . . I may be here some time. Sergeants don't do any work here at all. The weather is lovely, just like summer.' He asks his mother to send him cigarettes, soap and food parcels, but asks just as keenly for letters, to assuage his loneliness: *'try and make it a habit for someone to write every week. I am so lonely dear Mother.'*

In a touching and affectionate letter sent to his wife six months later in October 1918, Stanley gives fewer details about his life in the camp at Gardelegen, and maintains a much more positive tone to support her: *'My Darling Girlie Nell, Just another letter day in the same old way to let you know all is going along splendid. I had a card from you last dated 2 Sept. Glad you and my little Sonny are still enjoying good health. I am having a grand time here. The weather is just like a day in June today. Not a bit cold. I am out all day.'* He does his best to keep in good spirits and urges Nell to do the same. *'I am glad to hear you get my letters and cards Nell. I hope you are keeping up your heart as well as your Hubby my Pet. I am sure wee Stanny must be a fine lad by now . . . Cheer up now Lovey. I hear it may not be too long till we are together once again, and you know what that happy day will mean . . . God Be with you my Darling and my little Son is the earnest prayer of your Affectionate and Devoted Hubby xxx Stanley xxxxxxxxxxxx.'*

He adds a PS: *'I never forget to pray for you Darling. Remember me to Uncle and Mother, Meg and all the old clocks at the Royle.*

Tell Mother all the news when you write and Uncle Andy to drink my health on 18 December.'

Adams' optimism paid off, as only three months later he sent Nell a pre-printed postcard announcing his arrival back in the UK. The card reads: I have just landed at Leith, and am going on to PRISONERS OF WAR RECEPTION CAMP, SOUTH CAMP, RIPON. Underneath, in fading pencil, is his signature: *'Stanley* XXX'.

Harold and Jessie Robinson

Private Harold Robinson joined the army towards the end of the First World War in late 1917. After a period of training with a third-line reserve battalion of the London Regiment he left for France and the Western Front in April 1918. Harold left behind his sweetheart Jessie, to whom he wrote regularly. Despite the fact that the conflict was entering its final phase, it would be eighteen months before he returned to marry his sweetheart, and during their period of separation he wrote her around one hundred and twenty-five letters.

Harold and Jessie were able to meet at weekends during his initial training over the winter of 1917 to 1918, but Harold still wrote to her on a regular basis before he left for France. His letters are wonderfully affectionate, and in them he is very open about the strength of his feelings for his fiancée: '*since I have* been with you I have had some of the very best times of my life.' He is endearingly honest about how happy it makes him to receive her letters during his training: '*I am in luck's way tonight as I have had three letters from one post. What a great thing is a letter, it works wonders at times and is far better than all medicines. For I was just feeling a little fed up as we had been all day on field work, and when we returned I saw your letter lying on my bed. Well needless to say all my trouble disappeared . . .*'

Harold's letters are full of charm, and often rather cheeky. Jessie sent her fiancé a watch for Christmas, and she must have been thrilled to receive his amorous thank you note in return: '*As for the watch I shall be able to look at its face and picture in my mind a face far better.*' At the end of one letter, after a series of pencil kisses he wrote, '*These do not make the lips sore. HR.*'

When Harold was posted to France in April 1918, to swell the ranks following the massive German spring offensive of that year, he joined the 1st/17th (County of London) Battalion (Poplar and Stepney Rifles). Just before sailing from Southampton he wrote to Jessie: '*You must excuse this letter, as tables and writing rooms are a thing of the past. We are now all sitting on the floor of a shed in the harbour waiting for the time to leave.*' He warned her not to be too anxious should his letters prove irregular in the future: '*For I shall write whenever possible but if you don't get them at regular intervals don't start worrying. Because as you know the army is rather unsettled at the present time which might mean that we shall get plenty to do . . .*'

Harold remained with his battalion during April, May and June of that year. His division took part in the Battle of the Ancre in early April, and his letters from this period hint at the shock of his first few weeks at the front: '*I expect you would like to know a little of what has happened during the first fortnight but I think it will be better for you not to know or you will be dreaming about France.*' Shortly after this the battalion moved to a '*quiet farming village well behind the line*' and settled down to a few weeks of training and cleaning of equipment. It took a few more days before Jessie's letters from England began to reach him, but when they did, he found them immensely comforting: '*At last they are coming through and it seems like England once again.*' As well as her letters, Harold also put a great deal of value on having Jessie's photograph: '*it cheers me up very much to glance at your photo.*'

In May Harold was back up the line, but a birthday message he sent Jessie made light of his service in the trenches. '*Yet you may be sure I shall be thinking of you more than ever on the 7th and wishing that I could be with you, instead of playing at mud pies,*' he joked. His next letter, however, reveals the depth of Jessie's anxiety for his safety. '*I have just had your brother's letter and he tells me you are worrying yourself too much . . . you must try and cheer up, for life is sweet and we must make the best of it while we can.*'

Harold had few chances to write during the latter part of May as his battalion moved from village to village, sleeping in the open, but Jessie's letters always seem to have found him. '*Post is a great thing in France as I have said before, no matter where the battalion is moved to, whether in the trenches or cellars, the postman follows us up.*' Her letters seem to have helped immensely in keeping his spirits up: '*It has been a very great comfort to receive a letter from you so often and to know that not even in a few idle moments that I am out of your mind. I often think of the time we have had together and wish that I could be back again with you and spend all those happy days over again. All this we owe to the Bosche yet we must watch the clock and wait for the time when this beastly game is over ...'*

Harold continued serving in the front line during June, exposure to the trenches enhancing still further his appreciation of the solace that letter-writing could bring:

'I am so pleased that my letters bring you so much comfort and you may be sure that yours brings equal amount of comfort to me. It is true that the pen is mightier than the sword or any other weapon of war. I don't know how we should get on, if we were not able to get a line from home. The first thoughts of a Tommy when in a tight corner, is the dear ones at home. Only last night I heard one poor chap crying for his mother, it's a terrible war as one sees it in France.'

In July he was hospitalized with influenza. A few days later he wrote to Jessie assuring her that he was on the mend: *'Well I have had a very good rest and I feel quite ok to take up the old game again and see if we can finish off this old war.'* He remained in hospital for a month, however, from where he wrote, *'it is a real pleasure to be away from the noise of the guns.'* It did not take long before he had recovered his cheeky nature: *'No doubt you would like to get a glimpse of me (especially in shorts) but I don't think they have started making passenger trips by aeroplane.'*

On his release from hospital he did not return to his battalion, transferring instead to a convalescent camp in Rouen, where his light duties included playing in the band. He enjoyed a relaxing few weeks exploring Rouen, visiting the theatre and the cinema, walking around the town and even dancing, all the time regaining his strength. His letters during this period are full of the good news from the front: '*I think there are some very happy times coming and the more we see the paper with all its wonderful news, it makes one feel that the dear old home is nearly in sight.*' And when finally the Armistice was announced in November, he was exultant: '*how the joybells are ringing . . .*'

Harold originally hoped to be home in time for Christmas, but the demobilization process was slow and in reality it was many months before he could return. Both Harold and Jessie became increasingly frustrated at his long wait, but he often wrote in his letters how her love helped him through this difficult period:

'*I do long to be by your side again and the more I think of it the more intense becomes my desire to see you. There are times in the army when one is apt to feel a little down in the dumps, owing to conditions which he has to live in. But at such times, which are not very often, I am glad to say that the thought of you and the happy times of the past buck me up considerably, as I know I have one who does really care for me and whose love is true . . .*'

Harold left the convalescent camp to rejoin the BEF, and at the end of January he was made a policeman. His duties were fairly light, consisting of several hours on guard outside the general's headquarters each day. He moved into a billet with a French family, taking language lessons from the children. He remained in France all through the spring and summer, telling Jessie in his letters about the swimming, cricket, rowing, and trips to Boulogne he undertook between his police duties. In July he was granted leave, and wrote to Jessie on his return: '*It wants believing that only last night we were in one another's arms enjoying ourselves in the very best way and tonight we are miles away . . . I miss your beautiful soft lips today. I suppose you cannot send them out to me by the next post.*'

Finally in October 1919 Harold was demobbed. He returned home and married his sweetheart. In one of the last letters in the collection, written to Jessie from his mother's house in Chatham in early October, he wrote:

'*My views are the same as yours, that I only love one and that is you . . . The soldier's character is like the sailor's, that they have a girl in every port or town. I have put this in, because some folk believe that all are alike. But no, since I joined the army, I made a promise that I would be true to you what ever happened. I have left the land of temptation and returned home safely and this promise is unbroken.*'

ALAN McPEAKE AND
EILEEN LINN

❧

Alan Young McPeake was an Irish-born London schoolboy who, in December 1917, received his call-up papers to join the army. After six months training with the Household Brigade Officer Cadet Battalion at Bushey, he was posted to the 3rd Connaught Rangers at Dover. Alan clearly had an eye for the girls and his schoolboy diary is peppered with references to them: '*Long love letter from Sheila, very much surprised.*' '*Una was in great form – at least so it seemed – I asked her for a curl* [of her hair] *but got nothing but refusals. Very nearly quarrelled*', and others in similar vein.

In Dover, however, Alan would meet his match when, as he noted in his diary on Sunday 11 August 1918, he and his friend Harry Mattison '*Met and talked to 3 girls, the first a nice*

Alan McPeake: one minute a schoolboy, the next an officer . . .

Eileen Linn.

kid from Ireland'. Writing in later life, Alan recalled their meeting at greater length: '*Harry and I were spending the afternoon on the hillside above the camp when three sisters came and sat down near us. They all had prayer books and Harry asked them if they were going to church. They said "yes" and in mock horror I asked "Not a Prodsin church?" Harry explained he was a "lone English Protestant in a camp full of terrible Irish Papists". After some more of this nonsense they departed . . .*'

According to his diary, Alan saw Eileen Linn five times in ten days, with Thursday 29 August a highlight: '*a topping night with Eileen*'. But the following day he received movement orders to join the 5th Battalion of the Connaught Rangers in France and it was then that he made his mistake. '*When I knew I was going to France she said she would write to me. I must have talked to her as Harry would have wished – not to get sentimental about young Irish officers. This made her rather angry and the only letter I got from her in France was ticking me off for not thinking she could keep her head.*'

Eileen's letter arrived in the trenches at dawn on 8 October 1918, just as Second Lieutenant Alan McPeake was about to go into action for the first time at Serain, near Le Cateau. Eileen made plain that she was annoyed at being patronized, but her annoyance was at least tempered by playfulness.

'Dear Alan

Thanks so much for your letter of the 6th inst. which I received OK yesterday morning. I am very much afraid you are labouring under a great mistake, for the "little girl in the green tammy" has no thought of losing her head but has just a great *interest and pity for a lonely little boy out in France ... You always seemed so lonely and fed up that I think perhaps I have sometimes taken* too *great an interest in the little boy.*

You are quite an expert at ticking people off politely. If it had been anyone else but you, I should really have been offended; but I suppose you receive so many letters from young females, who are just "ships which passed in the night", that you are absolutely fed up with them and it becomes a case of having to tick them off. If I have offended you in any way I am ever so sorry, for I can assure you I did it unintentionally.

If you were in "Blighty" I should have to ruffle your hair, for I am not a little girl any longer. You really make me quite cross when you call me "little child", etc., so please, little boy, don't do it again ...

As you say, I shall look back on this first romance (as you termed it) (but I am afraid it's not the first but the second: but still I'm not a flirt) but I am not so sure if I shall laugh about it. After all I expect I shall, for when you're sixteen you think one thing, eighteen another and so on, until you finally settle down ...

You must be absolutely sick of this "piffle", and terribly bored, so I must be sensible. I was so pleased to receive Harry's letter I have enclosed one for him as you will see ...

My sisters wish to be remembered to you, and now I must close so cheerio! The best of good luck to both of you.

Yours sincerely
Eileen
X for luck'

Harry Mattison in the uniform of the Northumberland Hussars, 1914.

For his part, Alan endured a torrid baptism of fire at Serain. Even at this late stage of the war the Germans could inflict terrible casualties, and in the course of four days of fighting the 5th Connaughts lost 700 men. Alan's friend Harry Mattison was wounded and captured; Alan himself was wounded and invalided home.

Once recovered, he saw Eileen again one last time: '*When I returned to Dover briefly before demob, we were sort of hostile friends – she was the "kid sister" sort, but we parted as real friends. I never saw her again. Years later she wrote [to] me. She hoped to go to Canada with a young engineer, and she could now say nice things about what she really thought of me. And she did. I hope they prospered.*'

Alan McPeake went on to marry another woman, Agatha, and lived until 1987.

EDWARD PRINCE OF WALES AND MRS FREDA DUDLEY WARD

❧

The armistice of 11 November 1918 with Germany brought an end to a frustrating war for Edward, Prince of Wales. Although a commissioned officer in the Grenadier Guards, his position as heir to the throne prevented him from seeing active service. He had been able to visit the trenches, and even come under shellfire, but his main role was as an observer at army and corps head-quarters. His father, King George V, had refused to countenance him acting even as an aide-de-camp, regarding it as incompatible with his royal status. So now, at the end of the war, and at the request of the commander of the British Expeditionary Force, Field Marshal Sir Douglas Haig, the Prince of Wales was visiting troops of both the Canadian and Australian army corps in a show of thanks for their contribution to victory.

HRH The Prince of Wales in the garden of the chateau that was his headquarters in France.

The Prince nevertheless had one consolation: he was passionately in love. In February 1918, while attending a dance in Belgrave Square, he had a chance meeting with Mrs Winifred 'Freda' Dudley Ward, who had taken shelter in the premises' doorway during an air raid and been invited in. Edward was smitten and, before he returned to France the following month, they were lovers. Freda and her husband, the Liberal MP William Dudley Ward, led largely separate lives, so a liaison with the Prince of Wales was not entirely scandalous, and it certainly gave Edward's rather aimless life a focus it had hitherto been lacking.

When he wrote to Freda on Christmas Day 1918, the Prince poured out his feelings for her. He was bored with meeting generals, fearful of getting 'boxed' (drunk) and, while professing sympathy for the desire of the ordinary soldier to go home – a forerunner of the concern for the common man which saw him famously state 'something must be done' when visiting unemployed Welsh miners during his short reign as King Edward VIII in 1936 – what chiefly comes across in his letter is a callow self-pity. Freda, who possessed a remarkably forgiving disposition, indulged him.

'Headquarters 4th Army
(Near Namur)
25 Dec 1918

My own darling sweetheart

Don't be worried by my address; I'm only staying the night here after dining with old Rawlinson the army commander and I return to Australian Corps tomorrow!! But I'm visiting the South African Brigade (66th DIV) en route: more propaganda, so it's not exactly a joy ride darling; in fact I've been too bored for words here to-night, a very nasty dinner with a lot of old generals who tried to pretend they were "boxed" and I had to play silly games afterwards!! That's been my Xmas, sweetheart, tho I don't suppose any worse than yours spent "en famille"!! How I loathe Xmas!! Yesterday I gave away over 100 DCMs and MMs to men of 2nd Australian Div at 3 brigade parades which was a quick way of seeing a Div tho of course more formal and not so good as visiting battalions in billets!! But I should never get thro all the billets in six months and I should be dead long before; you just can't think how tired I get nowadays and I'm stone cold after a few days of billets, so that I welcome these parades in a way, tho I've got lots ahead of me and close on 1000 medals to give!! What a life sweetheart, tho as usual I have to check myself and say enough about my rotten self! I had to go round the men's messes this morning and wish them a "Merry Xmas" knowing the whole time what rot I was talking and that the men thought so still more; who cares a d— about Xmas or anything else nowadays; it's only "home" that anybody thinks about!!

I'm getting just a teeny bit worried over your long silence, belovèd one . . . I haven't had a letter since 16th Dec and of course I'm too miserable for words!! However I must be patient and feel sure I shall find the longed-for envelope addressed in the only hand-writing that I ever want to see on my return to Australian Corps tomorrow . . . Please forgive your E for being such a bore sweetheart, only you know how hopelessly and madly he's in love with

Headquarters 4th Army
(near NAMUR)

25th Dec. 1918

My own darling sweetheart. Don't be worried by my
address; I'm only staying the night here after dining
with old Rawlinson the army commᵈʳ & I return to
Australian Corps to-morrow !! But I'm visiting the
South African Bde (66th Div.) en route, more
propaganda so its not exactly a joy ride darling;
in fact I've been too bored for words here to-night,
a very nasty dinner with a lot of old generals
who tried to pretend they were "bored" & I had to
play silly games afterwards !! That's been my Xmas
sweetheart tho. I don't suppose any worse than
yours spent "en famille" !! How I loathe Xmas !!
Yesterday I gave away over 100 D.C.M's & M.M's.
to men of 2nd Aust. Div. at 3 brigade parades
which was a quick way of seeing a Div. tho. of
course more formal & not so good as visiting battⁿˢ
in billets ! But I should never get thro. all the
billets in 6 months & I should be dead long before;
you just can't think how tired I get nowadays
beloved one & I'm stone cold after a few days of
billets so that I welcome these parades in a way tho.
I've got lots ahead of me & close on 1000 medals to
give !! What a life sweetheart tho. as usual I have
to check myself & say enough about my rotten self;
I had to go round of the men's messes this morning
& wish them a "merry Xmas" knowing the whole time
what rot I was talking & that the men thought so
still more; who cares a d— about Xmas or anything
else nowadays; its only "home" that anybody thinks
about !!

HRH The Prince of Wales to Mrs Freda Dudley Ward.

Toi, *so that you can imagine what an effect 10 days* "sans lettre" *has on him!! So long as my belovèd little girl isn't ill I'm not worrying as I know she loves* Moi *just a little bit; still it's most fearfully depressing tho. I wont say any more and feel such a — for having said a word about it at all and it's probably all very unjustified!! Like* Toi *has said to me just a teeny bit of paper with your signature belovèd one suffices!!!!*

I wish I had some news as my letters are so so *deadly nowadays and I'm so sorry sweetheart, but guess one doesn't hear much at the Australian Corps [where] the only form of amusement is to get* "boxed" . . . *needless to say I look on darling, tho I laugh a lot!! One has to enter into their life and amusements as much as one can when one is living with them, tho I fear getting* "boxed" *as it always makes me feel so ill!! However I'm nearing the end of this fearful existence* . . . *I'm quite looking forward to a week on the Rhine in about a fortnight, tho of course I'll give you my plans in detail when they are fixed. I think and hope 1st week in Feb should see me back to England and* Toi *sweetheart if you'll have* Moi *who dreams and thinks of nothing and no one else; your E's love and adoration of* Toi "passeth all understanding" *and that's more than the truth!!*

Good night and "dors bien" *my very own darling belovèd little girl. Penses quelquefois à ton petit E qui t'embrasse de tout son Coeur et qui t'appartient de plus en plus entièrement.**

Bless you my sweetheart Thine *E'*

* *Think sometimes of your little E who embraces you with all his heart and who belongs to you entirely more and more.*

Mrs Dudley Ward, who did not divorce her husband until 1932, remained the great love of the Prince of Wales' life until he finally broke with her two years later. By that time, 1934, Mrs Simpson had appeared on the scene.

Reg Bailey and Hilda Gower

Sergeant Reginald 'Reg' Bailey joined the army in 1908, aged sixteen, and served with the East Kent Regiment, or 'The Buffs'. When the First World War broke out he fought at Gallipoli in 1915, was wounded and convalesced in Brighton. Before he was sent overseas again he was billeted with the Gower family at Number 1 Colenso Villas, Tonbridge, Kent. Here he struck up a friendship with one of the daughters of the household, Hilda, a nursing auxiliary.

In January 1917 Reg was posted to India, where a number of the army's Territorial Force units had been sent to relieve regular regiments for service in Europe. Once there, Reg joined the 1st/4th Buffs and over the following thirty months was stationed variously at Ranikhet, Bareilly and Multan. Over time the letters that he sent home to Hilda become increasingly

Reg Bailey in India, October 1917.

Reg (far right) convalescing in Brighton in 1915. Note the handwritten
caption on the postcard, which reads: 'Britons Noble Heroes'.

familiar until, on 5 October 1918, he felt able to cease addressing her as 'Dear Miss Gower'.

The earliest letters repeat well-worn in-jokes about broken
dishes, lounging on a sofa and her keeping polished a silver-
topped stick that he had left behind. '*That photo of you adorns
my bunk wall. When I see it, I always think of the preparation for
Xmas 1916 and the things you called me during that period, also
the dish* YOU *broke.*'

Similarly, on 14 October 1917 he wrote: '*I should like to pay
a surprise visit to that Hospital room, tongues wagging and tea dis-
appearing, oh yes. I know, don't get wild, but that sofa has not been
allowed to get cold lately, has it? Send me a photo of yourself in uniform or else get it in the Press. Thanks for wishing me back again,
but do you think you could stand it? I don't mean that* I *did all the*

talking (smile again). You spoil the compliment by writing about my "little" feet, when will you improve . . .'

And again, on 6 November: *'I guess you are full up with work now and I should like to know by return how many dishes you have broken up to date. Do you still wipe your floury hands on people's faces? My word, what I had to put up with, a poor weakling, in fact a "mere man", if I may say so. However I got over it all right and could do with the chance to help do that mincemeat now, I can tell you. I am wondering where we shall spend our Xmas; wherever it is, you can bet that we shall all be thinking of you at home. I hope you will have a jolly fine time; if I was about Tonbridge I would call in for that stick which you say comes in very useful for beating carpets.'*

By January 1918, and a year away from England, Reg was beginning to miss female company (at least the type that would deign to consort with soldiers). He could still be light-hearted about it, however:

'You still seem to enjoy yourself and I guess there is something doing in No. 1 now you have your sisters there. I reckon I should have a terrible life if I were there now, shouldn't be able to get a word in edgeways. I used to get a sentence in now and again, didn't I? (That was when you were out or were eating all the nuts!!) Now for a few minutes my ears will burn I guess. Am sorry you have nobody to help you shopping or to take you to see the pictures; there are no ladies here who care to go shopping with soldiers. They consider themselves far above us: what a shock they would get if they were to come home. Fancy having to do all their own housework instead of getting a native to do it – I smile up my sleeve at them, and the

airs and graces they have towards us; and likewise steer clear of them. I leave the job of looking after the ladies of the station to the young fellows! ahem; they will be like me later on – learn better, experience always teaches.'

Despite the flirtatious content of their letters, Reg did not imagine that he had sole claim on Hilda's affections. Occasionally he made jokey references to her boyfriends: '*I am sorry to see that you are going in for breaking people's hearts; do take care you don't come a cropper, and look here, you broke that dish, so don't say any more about it, I have said so and that's the finish.*' The news in June 1918 that an army camp was to be opened nearby gave him the opportunity for another dig: '*Guess Tonbridge will look up with 8000 Tommies in the town, hope they don't set the place alight too many times. Be careful now, and just because you say you have a piece of stone or ice in the place where your heart should be, don't imagine that ice does not melt . . . and even stones get lost or broken, so don't tell the old tale to me. I know, go easy Miss H or you will ride for a fall.*'

Reg was sometimes glad of his bachelor state: '*You would be surprised if you knew the number of fellows out here, and in our Mess too, whose girls have thrown them over and who have nobody to meet them. Every mail there seems to be one case of that sort of thing. I am rather pleased I am free or I might have the same happen to me.*'

He was aware that, while he was away, things were changing at home and the news that women had been granted the vote could not pass unremarked. He had not realized, unfortunately, that only women over thirty were eligible. When Hilda pointed this

out, Reg was mockingly contrite: '*I am sorry about that vote business, I had no idea that one had to be over 30 to get one (what would
you have said if I had suggested you had 2!!!!!!!). Am sure you don't
look anything like 30. My word, don't I put my foot in it.*' Nor could
he resist signing off with a tongue-in-cheek word of warning: '*I
have no doubt that, with all these years of freedom and we boys away,
you girls are getting independent. We will soon cure you of that.*'

The war in Europe was now finished, but by the spring of 1919
India itself was threatening to become a war zone. There was
nationalist agitation in the Punjab and in May the Afghans
invaded. Reg informed Hilda of the precautions being taken: '*I
expect you have heard all about the trouble here, it is a nuisance.
First it was the Rowlatt Bill in the Punjab and now the Afghans are
causing heaps of work and trouble. Everybody this way is mobi-
lizing, our people are standing by and some sixty have gone to
Ferozepore . . . We are evidently massing some army on the Frontier,
fellows who were going home from Mespot [Mesopotamia] are being
brought here, some were two and three days at sea, fancy, on the
way home for demobilization and then the ship turns around and
one has to spend some months on the frontier.*'

Multan, from where Reg wrote, was dangerous enough at the
best of times: '*I am glad you got the photos OK. Yes, the Railway
Station is about the best thing in Multan. I have never seen any of
the dancing women here, they are in the city and it is hardly advisable to venture down there except with an escort of Lewis guns.*'

The following month Reg had to react to news from Hilda that
he had an admirer:

Multan, where Reg was stationed in 1918. He wrote:
'My outlook upon the world is the four fort walls, beyond that sand
and trees, trees and sand, then more sand ...'

'*Great Scott, Good Heavens, ETC. ETC. ?* ?* ?** ? Fancy one of
your friends falling in love with my photo, didn't you tell her all
about me ...? Good thing she did not see me, or perhaps it would
be better if she did, she would not fall in love with the real article ...
If she takes it into her head to write to me, well, I guess I shall have
to answer it ... I am getting staid, and gradually losing my reason,
another year and I shall be right in the rats, if we stop here. I guess
I shall be absolutely lost when I get into a girl's company again.*'

By August, Reg could begin to look forward to repatriation,
warning Hilda in one of his final letters from India that there
would be more of him than she remembered: '*See here MISS, I
do not want so much of your old back chat about my being a staid*

Dancing Girl, Mooltan. (Meerasu.)   M. Dadabhoy, Photo., Mooltan.

One of Multan's dancing girls, whom Reg
claimed he never saw.

old gentleman. And if your friend has fallen in love with me, well,
you will not see me anywhere near Tonbridge WHEN I come home.
The best thing though, on second thoughts, to do, would be to come
straight there off the boat, then let your friend see me as I really am.
THAT would just about put the lid on things OK, poor girl, she
would be disillusioned. Fancy me, 12 to 14 stone, 40 odd round
the . . . chest, thought I was going to say tummy didn't you. Fat and
awkward, and too slow to catch a cold. There, tell your friend that.'

Reg was recalled to the Army in 1939 on the outbreak of the Second World War and was demobilized a second time in 1945. Sailing for France aged 52 in 1944, he wrote home: 'They must be short of men to send grandpas out . . .'

In spite of Reg's self-deprecation, Hilda liked what she saw and upon his return they married. Reg was demobilized in 1920, re-enlisting with the Buffs as a Territorial in 1925 and serving on until 1930. Between 1935 and 1939, as part of the supplementary reserve, he did a further four years in the Royal Army Pay Corps before being recalled on the outbreak of the Second World War and serving with the Royal Signals in North-West Europe in 1944–45.

THE SECOND WORLD WAR

1939–1945

HOME FROM DUNKIRK

As every schoolboy used to know, the end of the First World War by the Treaty of Versailles in 1919 contained within itself the seeds of a second, even greater conflict. 'This is not a peace. It is an armistice for twenty years,' Marshal Foch had declared; and so it proved. Self-determination for all European nations apart from defeated Germany was not the basis for a lasting settlement, and the Germans' sense of grievance was one which Adolf Hitler's Nazi Party, after it came to power in 1933, ruthlessly exploited. Hitler's opportunist annexations of Austria and Czechoslovakia were followed by an attack on Poland in September 1939, provoking Britain and France in turn to declare war on Germany.

The outbreak of the Second World War found the British Army small and unprepared. The army of its French ally was larger but handicapped by adherence to outmoded military doctrines. Neither could resist the German Army when it unleashed its blitzkrieg in the west in May 1940. The French front was pierced, the German armoured columns broke through to the English Channel, and the British Expeditionary Force (BEF) on the Continent was pressed back against the coast at Dunkirk. Evacuation of the BEF by sea was the only hope.

Operation Dynamo, which saw 338,000 British and French troops rescued from open beaches, seemed such an improbable event that it was immediately dubbed a 'miracle'. The very fact that there was nothing preordained about its success made the anxiety of those back in Britain, desperate for news of loved ones with the BEF, all the greater. Gratifyingly, the authorities realized the need for reassurance to be conveyed home as quickly as possible, as Private Allan Barratt of the 2nd Survey Regiment, Royal Artillery, having landed at Margate, recalled:

'We were led off along the promenade, where we boarded buses to take us to the railway station where a makeshift canteen had been set up, with trestle tables piled high with sandwiches and buns and mugs of tea, and we were told to 'get stuck in, lads'. We were given bars of chocolate and cigarettes (where from I don't know!). Also handed cards and told to address them to our next-of-kin with some message such as "Home safely", sign them, and the postcards would be delivered free to our folk at home. How wonderful, we thought, and how well organized. We were amazed at the reception given to an army which had just been kicked out of France!'

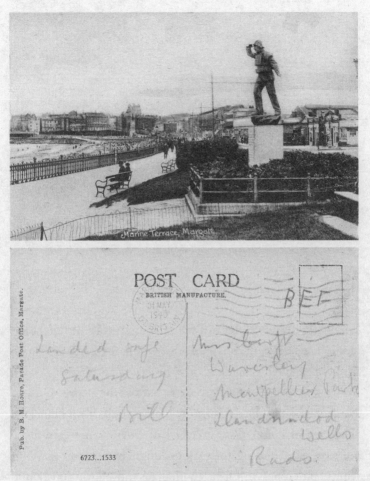

The postcard sent by William Croft to tell his wife of his return from Dunkirk.

Rarely could the arrival of a mundane seaside postcard, such as the example illustrated sent from Margate to his wife by William Croft of the Royal Army Ordnance Corps on 31 May 1940, have been received with such an overwhelming sense of relief.

Reggie and Myrtle Savory

Following the surrender of France in June 1940 Britain stood alone. The victory of the Royal Air Force in the Battle of Britain saved the United Kingdom from invasion, but there appeared little scope for the country to strike back at the enemy. Only in North Africa did the opportunity present itself. With France on the verge of defeat, Fascist Italy had entered the war on the German side, hoping for easy pickings. In September 1940, from their colony in Libya, the Italians moved cautiously into British-occupied Egypt. Prime Minister Winston Churchill, in a bold stroke, rushed tanks – which would have been desperately needed in the event of a German invasion – from Britain to Egypt to bolster the garrison there. The defence of the Suez Canal, and with it imperial communications with British possessions in the East, could not be jeopardized.

Reginald Savory.

As in the First World War, Britain to a great extent relied on troops drawn from its overseas empire to defend British interests abroad. Among the troops in Egypt was the 4th Indian Infantry Division, with one of its three brigades – the 11th – commanded by Brigadier Reginald Savory. 'Reggie' Savory had been commissioned into the Indian Army in 1914. During the First World War he served at Gallipoli and in Mesopotamia, before going to Siberia as part of the ill-fated allied intervention against the Russian Bolsheviks at the war's end. In 1922, aged twenty-eight, he married Myrtle Richardson. The couple remained in India between the wars, until Reggie parted from Myrtle to take up his command in March 1940. She returned to England to the family farm.

From Egypt Reggie wrote her affectionate letters until, on 19 December 1940, he had dramatic news to impart about his role in the British counter-offensive against the Italians at Sidi Barrani. Thirty thousand British and Indian troops had attacked 80,000 Italians. Victory was total: the Italians possessed no answer to the heavily armoured British Matilda tanks and the élan of the Indian soldiers.

'My beloved Girl,

Two days ago, I returned from ten hard days in the desert during which we fought and won a battle which will surely become historic. You will have read of it in the papers long before this letter can possibly reach you.

I know you will be interested when I say that my lot of merry men played no mean part. In fact we had the honour of opening the battle and upon our success depended the whole issue. It was a great responsibility. Anyhow we rattled along in the early dawn at such a pace and took the enemy so unawares that in just over two hours we had killed or captured every single man holding the objective allotted to us: and the rest of the army passed through in and on. And after that we also joined the rest and were in at the death of the Italian army in the Sidi Barrani area.

. . . We marched across the desert for many miles, spending ten days and ten nights en route. The weather was kind to us as there were low clouds and some haze which hindered enemy air observation. It was an anxious time, as all preludes of that kind are bound to be.

. . . I remember trying to sleep one night while we were advancing (It was bitterly cold and pretty miserable) and hearing a sergeant nearby saying "My God: I wouldn't miss this for anything." So cheerful: so keen. I felt like Henry V, and prayed like blazes for the success of our arms: for the first retaliation by the Army: the first I hope of many: and the only prayer that came to my mind was "Oh! God of battles steel my soldiers' hearts: poison them not with fear: take from them the sense of reckoning of the opposed numbers." There was no need for that prayer: but I kept at it just the same.

And then the eve of the great day came. Our arrival at the last rendezvous where we were to leave behind all our impediments and push onwards into the night to reach the particular point from which we intended to assault the enemy. That was my *appearance, and the acclaim was about to rise.*

Babu [his Indian servant] *had accompanied me up till then . . . but there I left him. I gave him a final "chit" in case I should be killed: and gave him also a letter for you (dear sweetheart) which he was to send to you through John. I enclose the letter, darling: it is sealed and you must open it. It may be worth reading: written half-an-hour before we left. One day we'll have a smile over it together.*

Poor Babu started weeping, and then produced from nowhere one of those little cloth pictures of the Sacred Heart and pinned it inside the lining of my steel helmet, saying "The memsahib said I was to do this." Rather touching, I thought.

By then it was dark and off we went. That was an anxious time. Everything depended on nothing going wrong. The success of everything depended on me. Anyhow we arrived at our allotted place: got a couple of hours' sleep: and rested, very near the enemy, until it was time to start the attack at dawn. It was cold and rather dreary. And then came the first glimmer of dawn, and the great moment had arrived. I gave my final orders: and then, not long afterwards, saw an unforgettable sight: that of the attacking army advancing at great speed through the "gap" (which you may have read of in the papers) and going in various directions towards their respective objectives. I shall never forget that: a swift mechanized force rushing forward in the half light to attack an enemy whom we realized by then was certain to be surprised.

Thank God it went without a hitch, although we had our tense moments, and the way was clear for the rest to pass through.

The enemy put up some kind of resistance: his artillery was good: his tanks never had a chance: but little bodies of infantry fought it out till the end. Their General was killed, firing a machine gun. We captured some thousands of prisoners and all their material. You never saw so much stuff. There was a bit of a counter-attack but it faded away.'

Reggie's 'last letter', mercifully unused, read as follows:

'In the Field
8 Dec 1940

My darling,
It is now 5 pm. We do a night march starting in half-an-hour: and attack the enemy at dawn.
I hope we shall be successful. If so it should be a big victory.
I am playing a most important part. I pray I may stand the test.
God bless you my beloved. If I am knocked out it will have been

Reggie (centre, pointing) directs his Brigade's operations during the Battle of Keren.

in a good Cause: and a proper death for a soldier. Don't sorrow or worry. We will meet Elsewhere in due course.

Your devoted husband,

Reg'

After its success in Egypt, the 4th Indian Division was switched south to the Sudan, from where it joined in the British attack on Eritrea, part of Italy's East African empire. Writing on 22 January 1941, Reggie tried to provide Myrtle with a sense of the rapidly changed scene around him:

'I am now sitting under a very thorny tree in the African bush. It is hot, but not unpleasantly so. There are a couple of ostriches not far off, many guinea-fowl, and gazelle. The enemy too are not far off! So you may guess that I am in it again and well to the fore. Perhaps I have told you too much already, but after all I must tell you something sometimes, otherwise my letters will just not be worth reading.

We have travelled far and fairly fast during the past month and it has been an interesting time. We have seldom been two consecutive nights in one place: and the past week has been a hard one. This is the first spare second I have had except to sleep. The bird-life here is most remarkable there are more really beautiful birds than I have ever seen anywhere in India. The most brilliant things, and so tame. Such a contrast to the desert. There *there was no colour except the perfect blue of the sea, no trees, no shade and a limitless view. Here, it is only the lack of water which has anything in common with the Western Desert.*

. . . God bless you my darling. I will write more later. This is just to let you know that I am alive and kicking.'

By the end of March, once stubborn Italian resistance at the mountain fastness of Keren had been overcome, almost all Eritrea fell into British hands. Mopping-up operations continued throughout the summer, Reggie confiding to Myrtle something of his daily existence, amid fulsome declarations of love, on 26 June:

Reggie and Myrtle Savory (centre) on a tiger hunt, complete with tiger.

'I write these occasional little notes to supplement the airgraphs which arrive, I hope, regularly and to tell you how much I love you, and want you and miss you. But you know that already. All the same, I shall go on repeating it just because of the pleasure it gives me to say "I love you" and again and again "I love you", though the war may rage and appear to be never-ending; and I shall go on loving you my darling whatever happens and however long it may be before I see your dear face again. And I wonder how long it will be. But in the meantime we must just go on hammering away at the Bosch and go on thinking of nothing else.

... In my spare minutes I am reading Thomas Hardy's novels, and am now in the middle of "The Mayor of Casterbridge", a delightful yarn ... I sit with [the book] propped up against my looking-glass (the little round shaving-glass) at breakfast and read it and ponder over it and then look out over the sea, so near, and feel that life at the moment anyhow, is not so bad, and get semi-transported to the English countryside and all the beauty there is in it; and to you, my dear wife, and my home and my farm and all I truly love ... I am not really a keen soldier. Everyone thinks I am. If I were, I should have gone further than I have and been cast for almost any height in the military world. But you know so well, don't you, that really all I want is my own home and the beauty to be found in it and in my country and in the beloved wife who gives beauty to everything she does and touches and gives beauty to my life even at this distance. Thank God for you.'

Between October 1941 and January 1942, in the wake of the final Italian defeat, Reggie was Military Governor of Eritrea. The entry of Japan into the war then saw him moved to the Far

East, where he took command of the 23rd Indian Division. For the next fourteen months he faced the Japanese in Burma. Towards the end of this period, on 29 May 1943, he began a letter to Myrtle.

'My darling Girl,

I have been out all day today in my jeep visiting the troops and driving through torrential rain and over roads feet deep in yellow slippery mud. I find it quite exhausting, bumping and sliding about, but I enjoy it. I spend very little time in my office ... and it is keeping out of doors and moving about which makes me as fit as I am: though there are times when I feel that I am getting older and fear that I may look it. Babu is never sympathetic when I say I am ageing ... He merely agrees and says "What can you expect when for three years you have been almost constantly in touch with the enemy?" I think I must hold almost a record in that respect: and I am getting almost accustomed to having an enemy a very few miles off and having constantly to be watching and ready.

But the strain is always there and of course the bigger the responsibility the greater the strain: though in some respects familiarity does breed a measure of contempt. All the same I shall be glad when the situation clears sufficiently for me to get right away for a month's complete rest. If only I could persuade the powers that be to let me fly home. It should not take very long now that the coast of Africa is clear: but how I should hate having to leave England again. I don't think I could ever do it, unless of course you came with me. It is getting very difficult to bring wives out here: even newly-appointed Governors are having difficulty, so what can a mere Major-General do? But, if ever I am given an appointment not in command of an active fighting formation I will do my damnedest to get you out.

It is a long long time since we saw each other: but curiously enough I do not feel it that way: you are as fresh to me as if we had parted but yesterday. I can hear your voice and at times almost talk to you. You are . . . with me so constantly that I feel as if you were partly here in person. When I am getting tired and stale you encourage me. A personality like yours can never dim. I owe to you everything I have in life: and I have everything I want in life thanks to you, but you yourself are missing. That's the real rub. What a test of fortitude this war is. It is certainly teaching us all to value the things that matter . . .

Well my dear: here I sit writing by the light of my hurricane lantern with the moths, bugs and flying-ants fluttering around it, the crickets singing loud . . . and my thoughts go out to you at Woodburn, in the peace of an English spring . . . How I long to be with you: and to be able to forget the war and talk of other things, perhaps with my head on your lovely breast.

God bless you my sweetheart. Cheer up and keep going. We have won through thus far and will go right ahead through to the end.

Your devoted lonely
Reg'

Three years of almost constant contact with the enemy came to an end with Reggie's appointment as Director of Infantry in India. He was reunited with Myrtle during a period of three months' home leave in November 1944. Later he was Adjutant-General in India until the country's independence in 1947, retiring the following year as a lieutenant-general and with a knighthood. Although Myrtle's death in 1965 ended their happy life together, Reggie proved of too romantic a disposition to remain bereft. In 1968 he met by chance in a London hotel Marie Nikolaevna Zurabova, a Tsarist general's daughter whom he had helped escape Vladivostok in 1920, and had not seen for almost fifty years.

He married her a year later.

LEN AND SUSAN FLETCHER

Len Fletcher, who worked in the print trade, was called up at the outbreak of war and drafted into the Royal Army Service Corps. In June 1940 he was sent out to Egypt with the 11th Motor Ambulance Convoy. The entry of Italy into the war meant that the direct route through the Mediterranean was closed and Len went with the first big convoy to go to Egypt round the Cape of Good Hope.

He wrote from the outset to his wife of five years, Susan. We only have his side of their correspondence, but it is clear that Len adored her, and felt the heartache of their separation keenly. Susan was vivacious, and he did not want her to be unhappy during his long absence. At first he was pleased that she had plenty of social engagements to fill her time. If he felt pangs of jealousy, they were more to do with the fact that she seemed to be having so much fun without him than because he did not trust her. He did his best to suppress them, not always with success.

The delivery of mail from Britain in Egypt was erratic and if and when it arrived it was sometimes out of order. This could cause confusion, as Len had discovered when he wrote on 11 November:

'It wasn't till I had read the third letter that I realized who Charles was. You ask me what reactions I had from reading about your escapades. Well dearest I must say my heart had little flutters and one or two burns, but now I have found out it is Freddie H[—]s' son I feel a lot easier. It was just that first letter which seemed to be all Charles and not much about myself I began to get jealous. If only I had read your previous letters things might have been a bit more explanatory and I shouldn't have mistaken the name Charles for somebody else whom I particularly dislike . . .

Now I have got this off my mind I feel a lot easier . . . What amuses me is that his wife knows all about it. She must be even tougher than you. If he has taken you out all these evenings in a week when does he see his wife? I don't think you could let me do that, darling, while you looked after a baby. I shouldn't dream of it for one thing, but circumstances are different now that there is a war on . . . When I read how you are giving the suckers the run around I think it's time I came home and gave you a spanking and what fun that would be. Whoopee!

I do hope Charles is giving you plenty of fun. By all accounts he is, but as these letters are now in the region of two months old and it will be at least six weeks before you receive this, he may be miles away from

Twickenham and you might even have some other boy wasting his money. Good luck and good hunting, but go carefully. I don't have to tell you to be that, I know, but you are so devilish, devastating and wonderful that you might make anyone lose their heads.'

Len himself could be romantic when the fancy took him. After one guard duty he wrote: *'I was glad I had the half-hour guards as I just gave the time to dreaming of you . . . when I closed my eyes I could see you standing just as you were in your blue coat at Basingstoke. I was holding you just like Maxim in* Rebecca [the film of which Len had just seen] *and it was grand. How terrible it was to wake up and find that I was just holding a rifle and bayonet.'* In a later letter he rhapsodized: *'I understand you have a new green frock for the dance. Does it cling from breast to waist and flare out like a bursting flower? I'd love to see you in all your loveliness standing on a pedestal beaming down at me with all your exuberant joy, waiting for me to lift you down. How I could hold you so close and caress you, your lovely skin shining and your heaving bosoms pressing close to my heart.'*

In February 1941 Len's unit was transferred to the Sudan to support operations against the Italians in Abyssinia. Mail became, if anything, more sporadic than before. *'There is a rumour,'* he wrote in March, *'that some mail has arrived at a nearby large town, but whether our Company has any remains to be seen. Some chaps are just receiving telegrams dispatched from England in December.'* They could put up with the heat and the bad food, *'but to stop our mail is a lousy trick.'* Mail tended to come in batches, and shortly after this Len was able to report that five air mail letters

Len Fletcher looking relaxed on the bonnet of an Austin K2 ambulance,
the same type that was driven by John Mills in the classic Second World
War film *Ice Cold in Alex*.

from Susan had arrived at once. None, he joked, had been
opened, so the censor would not have been shocked.

A new innovation, the airgraph, promised to speed communication, and Len explained to Susan how it worked on 3 May:
'*To-day I sent you a new kind of Air Mail Letter. As there has been*

so much delay in post . . . I thought the best way was to send one of
these new-fangled letters. It seems a good idea as they are pho-
tographed and sent by plane in negative form, printed in England
and despatched to you. They are supposed to be delivered in ten
days, but I have my doubts . . .'

For some, however, news from home could be unwelcome, as
Len wrote to Susan in June with tales of his colleagues' marital
troubles:

'All around me matrimonial problems are the chief topic. Perhaps
you have heard me speak of Jack P[—]s, from Epsom. Well . . . he
heard his wife has got a lover. Jack was very worried for some time
about it all and not having any news for many weeks made him
unwell and he has gone back to base. Do you remember little
Mitchell? Well he has had the biggest shock of all. He actually
received a photograph from his girl of her wedding to a Canadian
soldier. She said she was sorry, but as she hadn't heard from him she
married someone who fell in love with her at sight . . .

Now you tell me about Harry. Well my sweet I am not surprised.
She [Harry's wife] *very seldom writes and I have an inclination*
that Harry already expects foul play . . . he is really down in the
dumps. I know why and it makes it so hard for me, and of course
he's very deep and won't confide in me. This is just as well as I
should have to be so careful as to what I said. I feel it so much as
she must be so very brutal to do such a low trick when he is after
all giving his life for her safety.'

Len made his feelings about infidelity plain: '*In my estimation*
it is the dirtiest trick a woman can do when her husband is doing

The 11th Motor Ambulance Convoy ready for action in the Sudan.

so much for her ... I often wonder what Harry will do when he finds out. He is a most hot tempered individual and I'm afraid he'd stop at nothing. You see we are going through a war, where life itself means very little; blood is an everyday occurrence with us. In our job we see the horrors of war, and can you imagine a man coming home to face such a tragedy that has been going on deceitfully behind his back? It will be terrible, dear, and I hope I don't ever get mixed up in it.'

Meanwhile Susan was still enjoying herself at home and Len was beginning to feel both anxious and reproachful.

'The blitz doesn't seem to have stopped you from going to dances and films much. I hope you are not taking too many chances ... The Williams bloke ... sounded very strange and you seemed to

have made a hit. You spoke of Alec being a Casanova, but according to these four letters you haven't wasted much time yourself. Harry seems to pop up on every page and I should think he has been spending a small fortune on you. How did you explain the situation to Alec? I'm still in the dark as to what this Harry is like, and when you stated that you were having seven nights out as he was on leave I was terribly envious. I seem to have had a rough deal in this war don't you think? ... In fact I almost want to sing that song "Remember Me", or ask what has this chap got that I haven't.

Dearest, I do so hope that when I come home I shall be able to give you all the pleasure you have been having. You must give me time to get acclimatized to this gay life again after so many, many months of the outside world where gaiety is almost a crime. Sorrow, heartaches and tragedies are all that we see and every patient we carry means somebody is going to suffer beside him. It's a cruel world, and war brings things to such funny climaxes. I do so hope that now we can see the end; the corner is turned ...'

By now Len had returned to the Western Desert where the advent of the German Afrika Korps in support of the Italians had tilted the balance of the fighting against the British. A counter-offensive was being planned, but even on its eve in November 1941 Len's preoccupation with the state of his marriage loomed large:

'At the beginning of your letter you seemed rather tired of waiting for me so long ... I know it is terribly hard but please remember it is just as hard for me too. You have been wonderful during these trying days and I do love you so for it. The way you have been

faithful to me and shown me the way you do really care for me is wonderful and I am so proud to think that I am still everything in the world to you. I am afraid that I have been just a little jealous of some of your escorts, but the open way in which you have revealed all the facts to me makes me feel the happiest guy alive, to have such a wife who can have platonic friends and still love her husband just as much.'

The British 8th Army's Crusader offensive commenced on 18 November 1941. A week later, Len still sounded reasonably cheerful: *'Hulloh darling! I have just written you an airgraph as I know you will be particularly worried just at this time as we do seem to be in the thick of a big battle right now ... I find I want to write to you more when those big guns keep boom-booming. Something seems to twang on the strings of my heart just like you do when I have a little crisis over you ... Guess I love you very dearly darling for only you and 18ins. naval guns can make my heart flutter like this.'*

A further letter three days later was also fondly expressed: *'I speak to your photo every night and tell you how much I love you and those lovely eyes look down at me and say "I know you do". Please believe me Susan, this is not pen talk but actually what my heart wills me to say. I guess that some days you did seem to fade behind a cloud and I couldn't get to you. I was so unhappy, and yesterday we had a glorious rainbow and your smile came back to me brighter than ever.'*

This letter, though, only covered another one which Len asked Susan to open when alone. It contained a *cri de coeur* which, even now, is painful to read:

'I have waited over a fortnight for this last letter of yours and now that it has come I don't know quite how to write and tell you how I received it. Please remember dear we are living through hell at the moment: as you will gather by the date we are right bang in the biggest battle of the war so far. I don't want to hurt you my sweet, I don't want you to think me hateful in any way but to be quite frank I was terribly jealous of all your holiday. Such a letter couldn't have come at a worse time really as my nerves are very naturally on edge all the time, and when I read of the whole week being spent in the company of someone whom I don't even know, can you try and understand from my point of view dearest, it hurt me quite a lot. Don't think darling that my confidence in any way has been shaken in you and I don't want to pull to pieces the letter and have a post-mortem on it all. I just want you to know, straight from the shoulder, as we have always given and taken, that I love you so much that I just couldn't take the thoughts of someone acting in any capacity for a whole week's leave with you.

Does this sound rather rotten of me, am I a pig and not my usual self? Perhaps I am not, and perhaps the strain of these past 18 months has suddenly crumpled up on me. But somehow I want to cry out and do anything to fight this aching pain in my heart that you are miles away and I can't feel the warmth of your loving care and understanding. I love you so much, I wanted you to be happy and have everything to make you happy and yet now I know you are getting it, I feel as though I am being cheated out of all the things that were so sacred to me.

. . . George sounds a very nice chap and I do so want to meet him. I think it was swell of him to do my [motor]bike for me. But please, Susan, don't ever let him crowd in my little corners of your heart.

Please don't let him get too much of a habit. I can't bear the thoughts of any one paying you so much attention and doing all those little things that have meant so much to me in the past.

I have started this letter four times, each time I have put it away and thought to myself that I am the silliest kid that ever lived and that I am making a fuss about nothing. But somehow I feel I must tell you how I have had to fight my inner thoughts . . . Try and understand me; try and think of how you would receive this kind of letter if I were the writer, and perhaps you too would say that Len, you are hurting me, and I know you don't really mean to. That is how I do take it really, but nevertheless I still feel as though I am having to share what to me is more precious than anything on earth. Could you, for me dear, try and make as many of your evenings with Biddy and Flo and only an occasional change to male escorts if you must?

Please Susan, try and understand this is the hardest letter I have ever had to write in my life. I don't want you to feel hurt my sweet, but you did say in your letter of 20 August these sweet words:

"Dearest, I was very upset to hear that my letters depressed you, although I can imagine a little how you felt. If I do go around a bit, I'm only passing the time till you get back. However, dearest, if you do feel badly about it please tell me candidly what you want me to do. If you want me to forsake the company of the other sex I'll gladly do it to set your mind at ease."

Susan, sweet, these were grand words, so grand I hadn't the heart to tell you right there and then that I would rather you tried to keep to female parties. But since these loving words you seem to have gone a little bit more and spent a whole week in the company of one chap whom I must admit has cost me more sleepless nights than I have ever had in my life. I wake up shivering and I can't see you, Susan. Just him, and I can't sleep for hours as it seems to be torturing my brain. Please, oh please, Susan try and understand me, I am so so unhappy. I've always tried to give you everything you wanted.

My dearest will you give to me this one favour that I ask? But darling if you can't I shall just have to go on enduring it as I couldn't possibly lose you altogether . . . You seemed to have gone so far from me, and you just won't come to my heart where I can talk to you and show you the misery through which I am living. I have got drunk, I have taken six aspirins at bed time, but still my mind won't rest and I have just got to write and tell you all about it. I hope to-night I shall have got some consolation that at least you know how I feel, and I know deep down you will sacrifice these things for me.

Please, Susan, don't be cross with me for writing to you like this. I wish I hadn't got to, but somehow I know you will write to me and say "yes". Don't write any more about the whole affair. Just tell me you will do this one favour . . . Already I can see you. Susan – Susan – hold my hand, I am crying I love you so and I must tell you all that's in my heart. You are my all, I just can't share one little bit of you.'

The difficult thing now was that Len would have to wait many months to hear Susan's response. It did not help that Japan's entry into the war in December 1941 saw his unit hurried away from North Africa to the Far East in a desperate attempt to retrieve the situation in Malaya and the Dutch East Indies. The

Have a good look at this!

Maybe it's the last good look you'll have in your life!

German propaganda leaflets dropped over Allied positions blatantly used sex to undermine morale and weaken their targets' will to fight. The reverse of this one spells out three possible futures: death, disablement, or surrender and life in a German prisoner of war camp, in which case 'you have a chance of having another "good look".'

"You Americans are sooo different!"

Leaflets such as this one (front, above, and reverse, below) sought to drive a wedge between British troops and their American allies, by preying on British soldiers' fear of what their wives and girlfriends might be getting up to with the influx of Americans back in Britain.

British Soldiers!

You are fighting and dying far away from your country while the Yanks are putting up their tents in Merry Old England. They've got lots of money and loads of time to chase after your women.

And what about you?

THE SURPRISE...

Changes in social attitudes and women's increasing independence meant that infidelity was much more of an issue in the Second World War than it had been in the First. This German leaflet uses black humour to tap into what must have been a constant nagging anxiety for many serving soldiers. Note also its implication that the war would go on at least until 1947.

The Allies also used sex to get their message across. This leaflet, collected by Captain John Hartopp of the Royal Engineers, was produced by the US Army Engineers in December 1944 to encourage units to use the latest maps, information about which was on the reverse (hence, 'Turn 'er over').

390 Bombardment Group of the USAAF were based at RAF Framlingham, where Heather Taylor met the airmen with whom she danced at the Framlingham Anglo-American Club. Between July 1943 and April 1945 they flew more than 300 missions, losing more than 180 aircraft and 700 men. Framlingham Castle, where Heather went on her days out with Rick, is depicted on this insignia.

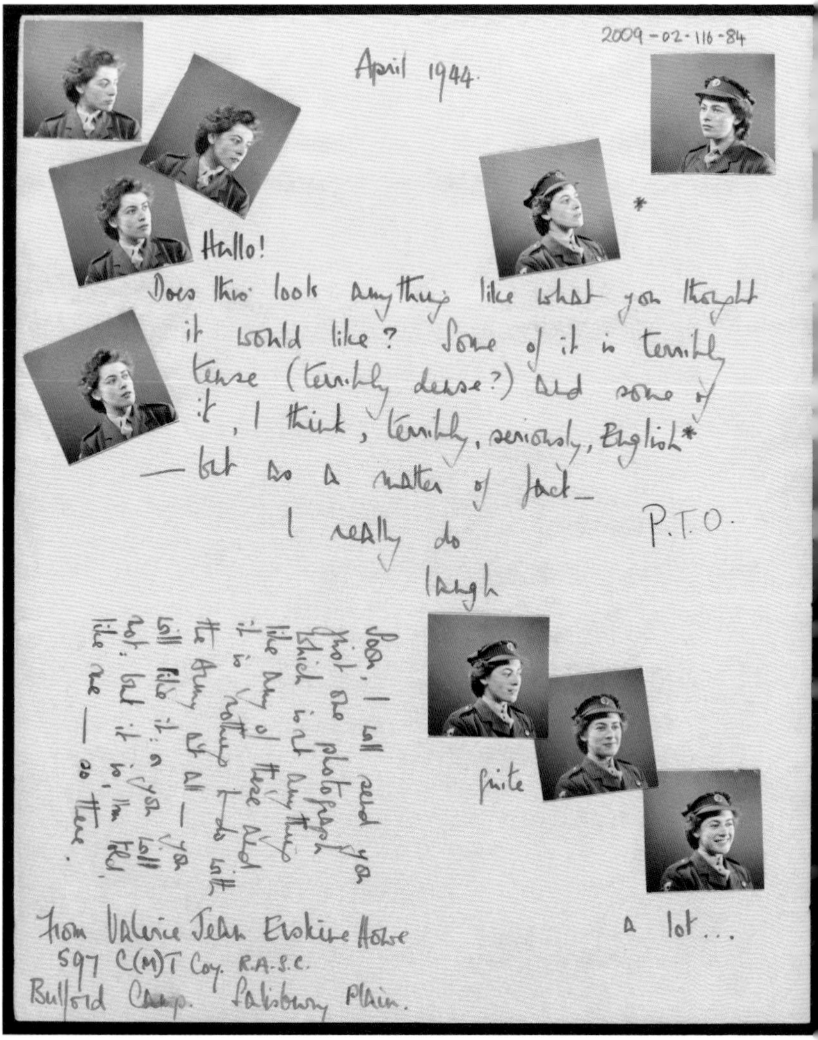

2009-02-116-84

April 1944.

*

Hello!

Does this look anything like what you thought it would like? Some of it is terribly tense (terribly dense?) and some of it, I think, terribly, seriously, English*
— but as a matter of fact —
I really do
laugh
quite
a lot...

P.T.O.

Soon, I will send you just one photograph which isn't anything like any of these which it is nothing to do with the Army at all — you will like it a lot: but it is, I'm told, like me — so there.

From Valerie Jean Erskine Howe
597 C(M)T Coy. R.A.S.C.
Bulford Camp. Salisbury Plain.

The letter Valerie Erskine Howe sent Anthony Ryshworth-Hill, full of her typical quirky style and humour, which, as he later wrote, made him decide to propose to her.

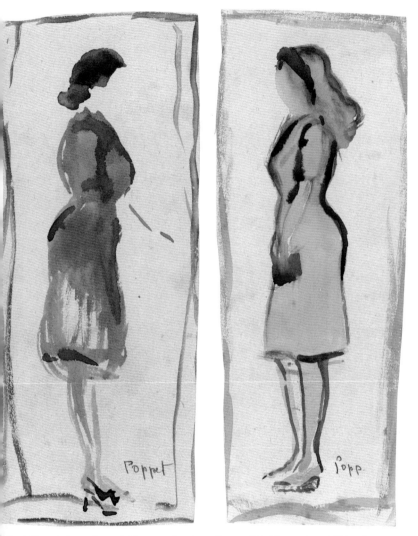

Nigel Gunnis kept these vivid street sketches of two of his Romanian girlfriends, Poppet (left, in red) and Anca Popp (right, in green).

Second World War correspondence was a much more monochrome affair than the romantic postcards which characterized the First. This card, sent by Major A. V. Shuttle to his wife from Burma in November 1944 and described by him as 'garish' was as colourful as it gets. The shields and insignia represent various formations fighting in South-East Asia.

Survivors: Reggie and Myrtle Savory, still a devoted couple in the early 1960s, almost twenty years after he wrote from Burma, 'God bless you my sweetheart. Cheer up and keep going. We have won through thus far . . .'

Len drew this pencil sketch of his wife in bed at the top of one of his letters.

fall of Java condemned Len to seven weeks at sea as a safe port of disembarkation was sought; in the end his vessel had to sail for India. Here he awaited news. Even by 22 March 1942 he had heard nothing from Susan since an airgraph of 10 October. A month later seven airmail letters, three airgraphs and seventeen postcards finally caught up with him at Lucknow, though not, as he put it, '"The Killer" letter'.

Finally, after nearly six months, came blessed relief. On 13 May Len wrote a grateful reply.

'... Although it has always been my policy to forget all the little regrettable incidents in life and never to refer to them again, your letter was so sweet I had to write you just a short letter in reply. All your love is in this little letter and although it may sound very sentimental I did sleep with your words under my pillow last night. The heading "Our Home" was very touching and I am sorry that

you shed many tears because of me dearest. Believe me when I say that any heartaches I may have caused you were not because I wanted to do so. If only I could have written the letter more gentlemanly, whereby I could have expressed myself without causing you any tears, then indeed I should have been happier.

My greatest worry was how you would accept the letter, and being so far away makes things so much more difficult than being able to take you in my arms and explain my feelings. Thank you for being so very sweet about the whole affair and although it really amounts to nothing, and I haven't lost one nth part of faith in your love and loyalty, I just couldn't bear the thoughts that temptations were in your sight. Everything about you, not just yourself dear, but your whole life and what you do is sacred to me. When someone jeopardizes your whole life for one whole week of pleasure I just couldn't take it. I do admire George for all he has done for you. It has been nice to know that your life hasn't been dull and that you have been able to escape from the misery of the war. But we sometimes forget in moments of thoughtlessness, for which after we are deeply sorry, that someone is feeling very grim when the pleasures are being robbed from the one person whom should be sharing them . . .

We have always told each other everything and I do thank you darling for being so honest about all that has taken place . . .

Thanks for the confession that you have admired me ever since I was a kid of seventeen. How I deserved to win you as my wife has always been a mystery to me. As regards the saying, "I got him girls", I would like to say that I would have moved heaven and earth to have got you, dear. I have always been so much in love with you ever since I first saw you . . . Now you are my wife and our love has *mellowed with the years. Many crises we have had to face, but by our understanding, sharing, and loving kindness we have and always shall win through.*

Your husband and devoted lover for always
Len xxxxxxx '

The two of them enjoyed a further fifty-five years of happy married life together and were separated only by Len's death in 1997.

HAROLD AND MARGARET
NEWMAN

❧

Britain's year of isolation in Europe, when it stood alone against Nazi Germany and Fascist Italy, had come to an end in June 1941 with Adolf Hitler's attack upon the Soviet Union. Ideological differences nevertheless dictated that the Communist Soviets could never be more than allies of convenience; and so ultimately of greater significance for the British was the entry of the United States into the Second World War following the Japanese attack on the American fleet at Pearl Harbor on 7 December 1941.

While the United States would eventually prove a mighty ally, at the outset the British were to suffer as much as the Americans from Japanese aggression. Malaya, with its strategically important rubber plantations, was quickly overrun, leading to the catastrophic surrender of Singapore on 15 February 1942. Not only that, the Japanese moved against the British colony of Burma, north-west of Malaya. Here the garrison was exiguous in the extreme and, despite the belated sending of reinforcements, here too the British were soon in headlong retreat.

Until this point, stationed across the Bay of Bengal in India had been 41-year-old Major Harold Newman of the Royal Engineers. He had married his wife, Margaret, in 1929, and she had lived with him in India until their return to England ten years later. The outbreak of war, however, had seen him posted back to India while Margaret remained at home. For Margaret, beginning a letter on 23 February 1942, there was dreadful suspense. Harold's latest of 1 January informed her that he was being sent away from Bangalore, but he did not know where. Margaret even so had a shrewd idea, commenting on '*the news from Burma, where now I feel convinced you must be*'. The fact that the news from Burma was uniformly bad naturally caused her anxiety: '*What it is to love anyone very dearly! One can bear separation when it has to be with a reasonably peaceful mind – for though one exists daily, one's mind is ever in the future – but put that person in any danger of his life and then the torments of mind begin, and it matters not how one endeavours to divert it with philosophy or work, or amidst a crowd, one finds the torment ever recurring! Then one grabs at every straw . . .*'

It was probably as well for Margaret's peace of mind that she did not know what was in store for her husband. He had indeed gone to Burma, arriving there by sea with the 17th Indian Division at the end of January. Initially Harold was sent to Taunggyi, to establish British lines of communications north

Harold Newman as a captain in India before the war.

towards Mandalay. '*I personally have never felt so isolated as now,*' he wrote to Margaret on the 28 February, '*not only from you whose latest letter reached me on November 27, but even from the world in general. No letters, even from India, have reached anyone in this entire outfit yet.*'

The loss of the Burmese capital, Rangoon, on 8 March forced the British to retire northwards, the evacuation of civilians giving Harold an opportunity to try and get word to Margaret:

'*This is going to be posted to India by a kind person who is being evacuated from Burma, not with the intention of evading censorship but hoping that the chances of its percolating through to you may be very much greater. She has also promised to send you a cable likewise. I hope you appreciate the kindness for I have no call upon her other than slight acquaintanceship initiated by an advert of hers for an exposure meter! ... Her name is Robbins. And that is practically all the information I can give you on that score. The poor people have to leave all their belongings, taking a mere 33 lbs of baggage, and have not the slightest idea as regards what their future may contain, or where it will be spent.*

... This frequent change in our official address is most aggravating. It makes one almost despair of ever getting any mail again. I took the trouble the other day to cable you our then address, only to find two days later that the field post office to which we had been told to refer our correspondents had been transferred hence. We have written to them asking them to be sure to forward anything arriving. What on earth is best to do? If I cable you this our third or fourth address, what guarantee is there of its permanency? One grows somewhat anaesthetized, especially during times of plenty of

work, to the absence of mails, but I am no dope fiend and not the least partial to anaesthesia. I have no hankering for further chloroform, and hope indeed to experience no further cause for it, either spiritually or physically.

. . . I should much like to know how the winter has treated you. Someday I may know, but the communication will probably be verbal – let it be sooner than later!

All my love for ever, H.'

Over the next month Harold finally received two letters and an airmail from Margaret, the most recent dated 25 January. But after 19 April he was not in a position either to send or receive anything. The retreat to India through Burma, the longest retreat in British military history (it totalled a thousand miles), was gathering pace as the British endeavoured to escape a succession of Japanese outflanking moves and the threat of encirclement. Only on 3 June, having reached India, could Harold send Margaret an airgraph confirming that he was safe.

'Bishop's House, Dibrughar, Assam

My dearest,

At very long last, after more weeks than I can count, comes the opportunity to write to you again. I am afraid the general news and my enforced silence will have given you cause for acute anxiety. There was no remedy to hand, we have been on the move the whole time since April 19, with nowhere a functioning post or telegraph office. This morning I sent an EFM [Expeditionary Forces Message telegram] *from here, but it has to be telephoned through a long way before final transmission, and I believe it is doubtful whether this or that will arrive first. As for receiving mails – well – the next to come will make a red-letter day for me.*

The first part of our trip might fall under the head of military operations, although we performed no active part ourselves; and it must suffice to say that for me it was a matter of driving a car, sometimes by night and sometimes by day, with once or twice a few days' halt, from April 19 till May 4. We slept under the stars or in huts, but we did have the luxury of bedding. The roads were mostly execrable, and we thought we were being tough. Little did we guess what lay in store.

On May 5 we discarded our remaining few possessions, everything beyond what would go in a pack or haversack (or both), which space

Margaret Newman, with fashionable white bull terrier.

had to include some scanty food, and hike it on foot, and we have been trekking ever since until four days ago, excepting for two days when a river in spate held us up. On full rations it would not have been so arduous, but, till about five days before the end when we encountered an organization of planters with ample supplies, we could only manage one inadequate meal per day. Often this consisted of mere rice and salt and tea without milk or sugar: latterly often mere hunks of slaughtered bullock. Lack of sleep too, due to sitting up though pouring rain, and to the merciless attacks of ravenous insects, and the fact that the track was mostly thick slippery mud, sapped our strength, and I am just a skeleton now as a result. We came roughly speaking due north from Myitkyina to Ledo in Assam.

So here I am, resting and hoping for some leave to recuperate my body, kit, and clothing (very little to be had here) enjoying the hospitality of the Bishop (a stroke of excellent fortune) and happily surprised at finding this airgraph system in operation. There are thousands in like case with myself, but now less comfortably housed. With all my love, yours as ever, Harold.'

Harold recovered from his ordeal and returned to Britain from India at the end of 1943, going on to serve in North-West Europe in 1945. He and Margaret were together until she died, aged fifty-eight, in 1965.

TED AND HELEN SENIOR

Harold Newman had managed to escape the Japanese by walking out of Burma, but not all were so fortunate. Ted Senior, a non-commissioned officer of the Indian Army Ordnance Corps attached to the 28th Infantry Brigade, was caught up in the débâcle of the Malayan campaign and found himself among over 80,000 men captured by the Japanese following the fall of Singapore on 15 February 1942. Three and a half years of imprisonment followed. At first Ted was held on Singapore Island until, in August 1942, he was moved by his captors to Thailand, where he worked on the railway which the Japanese were building to improve communications with Burma. The treatment meted out to the 60,000 Allied prisoners of war employed on the railway was harsh: the Japanese Samurai code despised men who, rather than embracing death, chose to surrender. In all, perhaps one in five prisoners constructing the railway would die from disease, malnutrition, neglect or deliberate cruelty.

Ted Senior kept a record of the conditions under which he was held in an illicit diary, written on scraps of paper. His entry for 19 May 1943, after he had been moved to Camp Number 8 on the River Kwai, reveals how much he yearned for his wife, Helen, who had come out to India to marry him in 1939.

'First chance of writing since arrival. Have gone sick to get a day off. A bad period. Work on quarries across rock face. Parade at 7.50 a.m. having a mess of soggy rice in the dark beforehand and return here at 7 p.m. or later. Often a roll call or other parade at 8 p.m. We usually just come up from the river in time to hear "Lights out". M[oreton, Albert] and I sit out on a log for a pipe – the one period we get of peace and then we have to take it from our sleeping hours. A lot of mail arrived on [the] 15th and I received 17 letters or cards from my dearest. All written in July or August 1942 – a year ago – what heartache! – she was being brave but it was a difficult business I could tell. A year has passed since then – where and how is she now? Deaths are very frequent here, 23 in 14 days – mostly British – a lot of sickness too. Food and conditions remain bad ... Life is pretty grim and the future so vague and uncertain – one gets very depressed at times ... I hope God will see us safely out of this before long. No leisure at all, no hope of writing any more poetry for my darling. I do think of her all the time and wonder if she can know anything of the dreadful time I have been thro and am still getting. I hope not, it would worry her to death. So many memories to help me, such a faith in my angel and our great love. It must end some day – God let it be soon. We love and need each other so very much.'

Ted Senior during his incarceration as a prisoner of war.

Helen Senior.

Ted, as his diary suggests, sought solace in composing poetry, when he had the opportunity. Some, following his liberation from imprisonment in Japan at the war's end in 1945, he had printed in a book, *Poems from Captivity*, which he dedicated to his wife. Others, such as the poem below, exist only as written; but all eloquently testify to the comfort that a man, enduring the most desperate privation, could derive from knowing that someone who loved him awaited his safe return.

'Memories

Murree, Clifton, Ghora Ghali – all the hills that lie around,
Memories so oft remind me of the joys in you I found
In those happy days of living (oh how far away they seem!)
Happy days and hills and laughter – turned to heartache and a
     dream.

Love was there in brimming measure, in Her heart and in Her eyes,
Love of my life to share each moment, make it all a paradise.
Sunny skies and cool hill breezes, trees and grass and eager stream,
Winding paths midst fern and flower – it was surely just a dream!

Rare retreats in which we rested; ringed with trees, grass carpeted,
Where we boiled our picnic kettle and round about our "table"
     spread,
— Happy days that in the darkness with a flash of memory gleam,

Oh my love that you might whisper – "Darling, that was NOT a
     dream!"

Ube, Japan. 1 November 1944.'

RICHARD AND JOAN POINTER

The British Army was not only in retreat in the Far East. Even in North Africa, where it had concentrated its efforts, events in early 1942 had gone badly. Recovering quickly from being forced back during the Crusader battles at the end of 1941, the Axis forces under General Erwin Rommel had defeated the 8th Army in the battles of Gazala and Mersa Matruh and, on 21 June 1942, captured 30,000 British and Empire troops at Tobruk. Although the Axis advance had been checked during the First Battle of El Alamein in July, Rommel planned a fresh attempt to break through to Alexandria at the end of August. To prevent this, reinforcements sent from Britain were rushed into the line with little time for acclimatization, among them the 2nd Battalion of the East Kent Regiment (the Buffs). One of those serving with the Buffs was 23-year-old Corporal Richard Pointer from Ramsgate, who had married Joan Hathaway the previous March. After a two-month voyage via South Africa, Richard's unit had disembarked in Egypt on 26 July, and on 8 August he sent Joan an airgraph to mark her twenty-first birthday. By 20 August, when he sent an airmail letter, the 2nd Buffs were in position on the front line under command of the 2nd New Zealand Division.

'My Own Darling Joan,

Hallo darling! Here I am once again all safe and well, and still smiling, as I sincerely hope this letter will find you.

... Well now to answer your two letters which cheered me up so much, it's just like having £100 given you, receiving a letter out here; they're so precious ... still I expect it's the same at home now, isn't it.

... I'm glad to hear that you were able to have the day off the other week darling ... I'd have given anything to have been with you. Oh! Wouldn't it have been grand, just like the last 3 weeks we had together. Oh! Boy, wasn't it lovely. Roll on the time when we can be together for always.

Now I'm afraid I shall have to close owing to shortage of space, so I'll finish off saying, keep your chin up and keep smiling, it won't be so long before I am home now.

So Goodnight my own darling wifey. Lots of love, tons of kisses, God bless and take care of you dearest.

Your everloving hubby.
Dick

I S[hall] A[lways] L[ove] Y[ou] Darling XXXXX
XXXXXXXXX *LOVE YOU DEARLY*
I LOVE YOU Dearest XXXXXX *'*

When he wrote again on 30 August the Battle of Alam Halfa was in progress. Richard alluded to it briefly.

Hallo! My darling, here I am once again, all safe and well and pleased to say that things aren't too bad; it was a bit noisy last night, but it's OK again now.

... Oh! Darling it was so lovely to hear from you again and to know that you are going on alright, it's like receiving a message from heaven receiving a letter from you now my lovely Angel! Oh! How I love you, more than anything in the whole world ...

... I only wish it could have been me instead of Janey who was having tea with you the other day ... still perhaps it won't be so long before I am back with you again my sweet. I do hope not at any rate dearest, because I'm missing you so much.

Now I must close, so Bye! Bye! My own darling wifey. Lots of love, tons of kisses, keep smiling and God take care of you dearest. Your ever loving hubby Dick'

Rommel's thrust had run out of steam by 1 September and he began to disengage. There was now an opportunity for a British counterstroke and it was one that General Bernard Montgomery, the new commander of the 8th Army, determined to take. The 2nd Buffs moved to prevent the enemy retreating via the gaps in the minefields through which they had initially advanced. In the heavy fighting of 3 and 4 September that followed, the Buffs suffered 108 casualties. Captain Ian Percival, officer commanding A Company, wrote to Joan Pointer afterwards:

'I knew Cpl Pointer very well and had great respect for him as a man and a soldier. He was very popular in his company and a good soldier.

At the Battle of Bare Ridge, 3 Sept 1942, he was commanding a section of the foremost platoon in a very exposed position, and it was then that he was fatally wounded. He knew no pain and was buried in the position.

You may be very proud of your husband, Mrs Pointer. He gave his life commanding his men in action, and has given us all an example to follow, an example one does not forget.'

John and Catherine Barr

The Battle of Alam Halfa proved to be Rommel's last opportunity to wrest Egypt from the British. Short of equipment and supplies, he was forced onto the defensive. Thirteen days of hard fighting between 23 October and 4 November 1942 then saw General Montgomery's 8th Army break Rommel's resistance at the Second Battle of El Alamein. The Germans and their Italian allies were forced to retreat back into Libya.

Just four days after El Alamein was won the discomfiture of the Axis was increased by Operation Torch, the Anglo-American landings on the north-west coast of Africa in Morocco and Algeria. The Vichy French, in occupation of these countries, quickly sided with the British and Americans, holding out the possibility of a rapid advance into Tunisia and the prospect of catching Rommel from the rear. Serving with the British 1st

John and Catherine Barr on their wedding day, 15 June 1940.

Army during the Tunisian campaign was Major John Barr, a Scottish surgeon of the Royal Army Medical Corps. He had been called up at the end of August 1939, when the outbreak of war appeared imminent and, like many others confronted by the uncertainties of wartime, determined to accelerate his courtship of his girlfriend Catherine Cunningham, whom he had met at his local tennis club. They announced their engagement on 15 December 1939 and married exactly six months later.

John's adoration of his new wife shines through in his letters. On 21 August 1940, while still stationed in Britain, he had compared theirs to the great romances of history: '*I don't know if you have ever read any of the world's greatest love stories. You may have seen films of them. I have and when I saw them I used to snort and pretend that it was all nonsense. Well, I admit to you that secretly I envied the hero and heroine and there was nothing I would not have given to be loved the same way. Darling, I am sure you and I are just as much in love as any of them, even though we are not likely ever to have a film of it; but perhaps someone might write about us.*'

When, in October 1942, John sailed to North Africa with the 11th Field Ambulance, he wrote to Catherine from aboard ship, whimsically rejoicing in the fact that, as an officer, for the present he could censor his own correspondence:

'*I hasten to send you this letter, not because I intend to break any of the rules of censorship, but I feel that I can talk to you much more freely as far as giving away information about how much I love you. I know the censor will let that through! Oh yes, in this case the censor agrees with every word. In fact, besides letting me say that I love you, he suggests that it is quite permissible to tell you that I think you are quite the most adorable wife in the world. He says too that I must not forget to say that I am missing you dreadfully.'*

He wrote to Catherine again once he was ashore and had an afternoon off. '*Naturally my first thought was another chance to write to my pretty wife and tell her I love her ... The other officers don't seem to write very often and when they do they never seem to write very much. Anyway they are always remarking how difficult it is to write a letter with everything censored. And one or two have remarked that I don't seem to have any trouble about writing. I don't say anything very definite to them in reply, but I feel that if they were as much in love as I am, they would have no difficulty. It seems that I am much "worse" than any of them.'* John did not normally admit to embarrassment on this score but was caught out a fortnight later: '*I was looking at your photograph just before I started this letter. I'm afraid one of the officers caught me doing so and I just didn't know what to say. I just showed him the photo and said "isn't she nice!"'*

By early December 1942, severe fighting had begun as the British closed in on Tunis and were met by German reinforcements hurried from Europe. John tried to shield Catherine from the harsh reality of war, writing about the improvement in his living quarters instead.

'I am feeling in a very romantic and reflective mood to-night. We have moved again and I find myself in a rather nice home. This room is rather darkly furnished, the type of room where you feel the silence descending upon you when you enter. I am sitting at a table

and the room is lit by the kindly light of a lamp with a mantle – much softer than the hard glare of the electric light. While I was sitting there considering what I would do after writing to Woully [his pet name for her] I espied a magazine – French of course . . . you would have loved it! All the latest Paris models – at least for 1939 . . . The magazine is called Marie Claire. *I liked some of the evening gowns. One in red which would have suited you very well – rather different from your own red gown, but very smart.*

. . . Strange seeing that advertisement [for a film they had seen together] *and how it brought back to me those happy days when you and I were just beginning to find out that love was such a lot to us: that we could not live apart. We found we both loved the same things, the same music, the same ideals. We had so very much in common. Darling, the dawning was so happy and full of promise. Then I thought of the future and how very much was in store for us . . . I am eager for the future, impatient and longing for all this to pass.'*

He ends his letter on a more sombre note. '*. . . Darling, I will say goodnight to you. I am tired – I had no sleep at all last night operating on these poor unfortunate soldiers. I prefer not to think of what I have seen this past 24 hours. No, I will go to bed and dream. I will come back to you and to our world for a few brief hours, but how refreshed I shall be.'*

Indeed, much as John tried to keep his letters uplifting, the nature of his work inevitably affected him. He admitted as much to Catherine on 28 December:

'*I am feeling rather depressed to-day, not so much personally, but rather depressed at the state of the world at present. It seems rather a curious thing to say, but what brought it to mind was an incident this morning. We had quite a number of casualties and most of them Germans. There were a few French, two Arabs, some British and some Americans – all in one "ward" and they all had similar symptoms and signs. The only difference was that they expressed themselves in their own language. Somehow it made war appear so completely mad and stupid. One of the patients I operated on was a German officer. He could speak French and asked me what I was going to do to his leg. I'm afraid my French conveyed to him that I was going to cut his leg off! I only meant open it up. He seemed quite alarmed, not unnaturally, but not so much at the operation. He was worried at the prospect of going home to his "jeune femme" with a wooden leg!! We calmed his fears. Afterwards while talking he said he wasn't interested in the war but just wanted back to his wife. It appeared he was newly married! So you can understand that I could sympathize with him in a way. Yes, all these incidents impress me every day with the complete futility of war, and I often think if the powers that be could see this side of it, they wouldn't be so keen. I am sure that so-and-so Hitler would have a fit if he realized the attitude of some of his "Soldiers of the Reich"!! Unfortunately they are not all like that so I expect we have got to go on until we have taught them a lesson.'*

One of John's major concerns was not to alarm Catherine unnecessarily. As a medic, he could expect for most of the time at least to be less exposed to immediate danger than a front-line soldier. Nevertheless on 1 December 1942 his commanding officer, Colonel Butcher, was killed in action, and John was placed in temporary command of his unit. At first he withheld this from his wife. But when the army raised his pay for the three weeks he was in command by the then princely sum of £20, he realized he would have to explain the reason for the increase in their finances. Besides, there had been a death notice for the Colonel in *The Times*. He wrote her a brief but telling account:

'Now perhaps I'd better give you some further details of Colonel Butcher's death. He was killed on 1 December about 11 a.m. He left me at the MDS [Medical Dressing Station] to go and visit some unit. Apparently when he got there, a small "show" developed. It didn't really concern him, but ... Colonel Butcher always tended to be a soldier rather than a doctor. Anyway he insisted on taking a gun and going out to see the "fun". He was killed. I am telling you this, darling, because I feel that you will appreciate that we ourselves were well behind the spot and not in any special danger. We were all sorry about it, but many of us did feel that he rather threw away his life.'

On another occasion he wrote to reassure her that although 'we as Medicals see a bad side of war ... there is a lot of fun out here too and we manage to get a laugh now and then.' That there was indeed humour to be found in almost any situation was something he had demonstrated when writing to Catherine a couple of months before: 'One rather amusing incident happened. The Padre was away for the day and one of the patients died just after arrival. I performed the Burial Service. Captain Gibson was to give the anaesthetic for a case I was going to do, and when the Sergeant asked if it was time to start, Gibson said, "Yes, Major Barr will be here shortly, he is just burying his last patient!!" I don't expect the patient on the table thought it was funny!'

*

By May 1943, the Germans and Italians in Tunisia were finally on the brink of surrender. The capture of 180,000 Axis soldiers there denuded Italy of troops to defend it, and the British and Americans, after an airborne and amphibious assault in July 1943, were able to take the island of Sicily in little more than a month. The invasion of the Italian mainland followed in September.

Writing on the 29th, John confirmed his new location. *'I have just been told that we can say in our letters where we are. If you received my last air mail you will have had no doubt that I was leaving Sicily and I am sure you must have guessed that we went to Italy . . .'* He tells her about the enthusiasm with which they were welcomed: '*When we arrived at each town we got a*

Italian townspeople welcoming British troops.

tremendous reception from the population, so much so in one town that I began to think we had missed the news that the war was over. What it will be like when the final armistice is declared, I hate to think.'

Yet in the midst of everything he still has time to think of gifts for her: '*. . . one piece of luck. We got to a lovely town which hadn't had many troops, with the result that there was very good shopping and the prices hadn't had time to soar. So you see I got a few nice things for my pretty wife. This afternoon I am going to a shop (not the same town) near where we are to see what I can do about lipstick and powder. I know you take special shades but I am risking a lucky guess. Will you send me as soon as possible* all *your measurements – stockings, undies, chest, waist, shade for lipstick and powder. I think we can get these . . . You could include your mother's shades and sizes too.'*

On 15 October 1943 John had been parted from Catherine for a year. He wrote to her reflecting on how hard he found their separation and counting the days until he would see her again:

'It is exactly a year to-day since we left Alva to join the ship for overseas. It was a dull bleak morning and quite the bleakest day of my life. I had said goodbye to my darling wife just the evening before. I had kissed her and looked into her lovely tear-stained eyes and I knew how desperately I loved her . . . The world had changed; it had suddenly become empty and meaningless. Yes, I had dreaded this day and it was every bit as bad as I had anticipated. In the midst of all that misery and loneliness I felt however a sense of relief.

The worst part of the war was over. From then on each day would bring me nearer to you.'

In fact another two years would pass before they were reunited. John served the remainder of the war on the Italian front, returning to his beloved Woully in 1945.

ANTHONY RYSHWORTH-HILL
AND VALERIE ERSKINE HOWE

Anthony Ryshworth-Hill was a captain of the South Lancashire Regiment and a veteran of Dunkirk who, in April 1942, was sent to attend a training course in Oxford. Here he met 21-year-old Valerie Erskine Howe, the cousin of a friend. She had only recently come out of an engagement, and over the course of the spring they became romantically involved. The two corresponded after Anthony was sent to North Africa as a staff officer with Operation Torch in November 1942; both were given to flights of fancy and wrote in a jocular vein.

As Anthony's admiration for Valerie deepened, he drafted in his diary the scenario of a play he had imagined, 'The Five Women' (i.e. the five women he had known in his life), in which the character sketch drawn of Valerie's *alter ego* read as follows: '*Jennifer, 22. Short, attractive, fresh looking (clean), swims, intelligent, well-read, mingled with undergraduates at Oxford (but no harm done), writes well, thoughtful sometimes, fey, moody, emotional, dresses colourfully, a good companion, loving. X* [his own character] *and J had some passionate months together and were parted by circumstance – both influenced each other a great deal.*'

By this time, Valerie had joined the Auxiliary Territorial Service, the women's branch of the army. Based at Bulford Camp on Salisbury Plain, she drove a Wolseley staff car, which she called 'Alice', and was also a dispatch rider. Anthony had returned to regimental duty upon promotion to major and when the Anglo-American 5th Army invaded Italy in September 1943, he was a company commander with the 6th Battalion the York and Lancaster Regiment. He won the Military Cross for his role in the breakout from the Salerno beach-head; although, in writing to Valerie, he humorously parodied his heroism, ensuring by the same token that nothing he divulged could alarm the censor:

"'Jenkins!"

"Sir."

"Have you wiped the blood off my Tommy Gun yet?"

"Yes sir, and I've cleaned up the Colt Automatic and dug the shrapnel out of your left boot."

"Good. Now get me some dum-dum ammo. Those last few Bosch I shot didn't die quickly enough."

"Sir. A letter from Lady Valerie sir."

"Ah. Take the body off the table and wipe those entrails away."

"Yes sir. You'll be having dinner at the usual hour?"

"Yes Jenkins. And bring me a pint of German blood to go with it."

Valerie as a dispatch rider: 'Anyhow it is fun on a motor-cycle ...'

All over Italy, they sing so prettily tra la la la, tra la la la! Well they don't sing where I am. It looks as if Satan, in a black mood had been kicking hell out of one of the filthiest corners of his ghetto. Unfortunately I was there when he was at work. However, birds sing now and people delve among rubble for belongings ... someone is going to give me a medal any minute – I don't quite know what for ... and a cow – which lived through a lot of stuff the Germans didn't live through – gives me a quart of milk each evening.'

Valerie, in return, teasingly tantalized Anthony with her own routine:

'Hullo – I'm FRIGHTFULLY BUSY – sh-sh – it is ABSOLUTELY CONFIDENTIAL – shall I tell you, it is SECRET. It is only that I should not really be here because I'm carrying Dispatches. They look AWFULLY IMPORTANT but one cannot help feeling that most of them are as important as so many rolls of — paper. Anyhow, it is fun on a motor-cycle: it is not so good when it rains, but then everything has its reverse side, and she doesn't wear things inside-out all the time, does she – no she doesn't.

I do about 117 miles per day – people are inclined to turn round and stare because "Gee – I say – isn't that cute – it's a girl." But when there are difficult traffic-jams it is easier to get through as a girl than as one of those bloody D[ispatch] R[ider]s!'

Beneath the humour, however, she makes it clear that he is never far from her thoughts, concluding: *'I somehow wish it was cotton-frock weather in Oxford and you would be wearing your corduroy trousers and – things. I expect I would spill the tea with excitement.'*

A couple of months later Valerie sent Anthony a letter plastered with small head and shoulder portraits of herself in uniform. The accompanying message was as light-hearted as ever:

'Hallo!
Does this look anything like what you thought it would [look] like? Some of it is terribly tense (terribly dense?) and some of it, I think, terribly, seriously, English – but as a matter of fact
I really do
laugh

Quite
a lot . . .
  Soon, I will send you just one photograph which isn't anything
like any of these and it is nothing to do with the Army at all — you
will like it: or you will not: but it is, I'm told, like me — so there.'

Judging by what Anthony wrote on the reverse some time later,
it was these photographs and words which decided him to make
Valerie his own. It did not matter that they had not seen each
other for over eighteen months and had spent such relatively
little time together beforehand.

'Darling Moon Child — this was my solace and consolation for long
months — almost a year — and always lived in my breast pocket (in
a new envelope from time to time) and later, much later, the poker-
dice joined it — I often used to take it out when I was very low,
being shelled or something, and look hard at it, and try and choose
which I liked best — and I used to say, here is my wife I hope, and
I hope beyond anything or any God anyone ever swore by — And I
loved the words on this because they were you, You — and I don't care
about whether it was April or May or anything but the words on
this meant an awful lot to me — because they were the sort of words,
well, maybe a Wife might write to a Husband, somehow. Even the
"so there"'

  Darling I love you so much — I love the silly hat you're wearing
and I love all your expressions — and well, I've always loved every
little bit of you, since, I believe, possibly since the pyramids were
built or perhaps a couple of years before.
  Anthony Husband'

Reunited: Anthony Ryshworth-Hill and Valerie Erskine Howe at Mallnitz, 1946.

Anthony's letter of proposal was penned on 22 May 1944 when, as second-in-command of the 1st/4th Hampshire Regiment, he was in Palestine at a Battle Training School.

'Hallo! I suppose you don't know where I am do you? Well I'm sitting on the balcony of a pretty big, but badly run hotel writing to you with hotel ink. There are two very comfortable beds in this room, one of which is unoccupied, and I wonder if you would care to stay with me tonight as I am leaving tomorrow? The wide tree-lined avenue below is thronged with guys and dolls taking the morning air, walking hither and thither with dogs on string, or pushing babies about. There are also taxi-cabs and horses and

soldiers and so forth. The sun is building up for a hot noon.

Valerie, shall we become engaged in a sort of distant way so that we are sort of linked together until we next meet? How would that suit you? This is not, as I said in my last epistle, the cry of the male buffalo from the lonely swamps of Mantrah River, as I am in the middle of civilization with all sorts of feminine attractions such as fat dolls, thin dolls, dolls built from the ground up, and ones very square and well hammered down ... In fact when I was cashing a cheque today a girl in a summer frock said to the officer cashier: "Hew did yew neaw that aye was an ATS officer. Actually eye'm on leave."

Somehow or other all these dolls and old buzzards rather repel me, and I desire to talk nonsense to you and help you to construct that baby which I think is a very very good idea indeed.

If you do go abroad which will probably be France please be careful ... I mean don't try to earn a VC or anything like that.

I am going to search for something you might like. I'm not awfully good at picking out things from the amazing mass of junk offered by the shops in this city. Anyway my income is carefully restricted by the Govmt. meanies.

"If I were a God
I would endow you with a star
And set bright youth forever in your limbs.
I am but dust
But no god loves as loves this poor frail dust"

Which is R. Aldington at random.
All my love and things
Anthony'

Anthony had chosen his moment well to propose. Valerie's response was ecstatic:

'Midsummer Day
June 1944
... evening

Anthony ... Yes, Anthony – shall we? I believe I would like it that way too. Somehow, to have put it into so many actual words startled me not a little. For a long long time now I have compared people I've met and talked to with you and I've decided within myself about a sweet indefiniteness with you more or less there – here, there and all the time – perhaps till the end of all things: but when your letter came yesterday morning I was late and in an instant hurry because I was detailed to drive Major X and he didn't want to be delayed, and there was your letter and come-wind-come-weather the whole war could pause a while for me to read it. And so I did – in the middle of the M[otor] T[ransport] yard – and – and you said – you actually said that! For 24 hours my brain has been in a silly whirl because I want it to be that way. I vowed ... that I would never ever again have a long engagement because of the strain of self-interrogation as the time swept rapidly by and the situation, amid countless outside influences, remained, in theory, the same. I've thought and thought until I felt rather sick (but I haven't eaten anything except dehydrated porridge (Airborne ration issue!) and drunken milk because it's too hot to think about food) and ... I've come to the conclusion that whether I am engaged to you or not that whatever I do or wherever I go you will always be to me exactly as foremost as you are now.

I feel very honoured – in the first place for the obvious reason and secondly – but by no means secondly in importance – because it seems that you believe in me to the extent of believing that I've somehow filled in the gap to make up the full percentage.

Dear Anthony – please God that you will not be disappointed . . .

I think that even if I was afraid of being engaged to you . . . our glorious strands of silver of god-like substance would have the same pull on our lives. I've said that before in this letter in another way. Hullo! Anthony-Anthony! I'm so frightened and yet so terribly happy.

Do you want me to announce this to the world, or what? I suppose one should, but if you want me to do it officially you'd better tell me exactly how to put it.

Hullo – do you feel any different? No – I don't either, I feel just exactly – just exactly – well now – well – I say, darling, it's a bit too crowded in here, shall we go down to the river and find a punt

"To Paradise for the sugar and onions
And we will drift home in the twilight
The trout will be rising . . ."
Oh Anthony!'

Anthony campaigned the remainder of 1944 in Italy, impatiently awaiting the time he could marry Valerie. In January 1945 his battalion, which as a temporary lieutenant-colonel he now commanded, was sent to Greece. At the end of the following month he was granted home leave and hurried back for his wedding, only to discover that Valerie was in an isolation hospital with measles. It fell to him to make all the arrangements and they were married on 2 March; their honeymoon was two nights in a hotel in Bournemouth. Anthony then returned to active service, and only when he was appointed commandant of the British Army's mountain warfare school at Mallnitz in Austria in 1946 was Valerie able to come and join him.

Anthony continued in the army until 1964, and Valerie accompanied him on his postings to places as far apart as Ghana and Turkey. After his death in 1984, Valerie remarried, but she and her new husband lost everything they owned as 'names' on the Lloyds insurance market in the late 1980s. Fortunately, Valerie's erstwhile fiancé, who had evidently carried something of a torch for her during the fifty years since their engagement was broken off, gave Valerie and her husband the use of a thirteenth-century friary, and it was here that Valerie lived until her own death in 2003.

THE AMERICANS IN BRITAIN:
HEATHER TAYLOR

After an initially rapid advance through southern Italy, the Allies were checked south of Rome by resolute German defence of the town of Cassino. This set a pattern. For long periods the Allies would find themselves held up before a succession of formidable German defensive positions strung across the width of the Italian peninsula, barring the way north. During these static periods of warfare, in hopes of being able to capitalize on their opponents' war-weariness, the Germans bombarded the Allied lines with artillery shells specially designed to scatter propaganda leaflets. Many of these leaflets attempted to turn the British soldier against their American fellows. United States troops had been stationed in the United Kingdom ever since the first contingent arrived in Northern Ireland in January 1942. A continuous build-up had then taken place in preparation for the opening of the second front in North-West Europe; by the spring of 1944 over one and a half million Americans were in England. 'Over-sexed, over-paid and over here', was the jaundiced reaction of many Britons at home, especially to the predictable need of so many men for diversion, and it was a feeling that the Germans did their best to exploit.

In April 1944, with the Allies stymied before Cassino and still no second front in France, British soldiers in Italy were regaled with various leaflets bearing the legend 'Indeed, an amusing war – for the Americans'. One of them went on to ask: 'By the way, old chap, did you ever think it over why the "inexhaustible reserves in manpower" of America have not turned up yet in this war?' The reason, claimed the leaflet, was not simply that the Americans were thought insufficiently trained to match Germany's superior troops, but that they were having too good a time in England. True, the anecdote employed to illustrate this, in which a woman in London – returning from the pub after getting a pitcher of beer for her 'old man' – is sexually assaulted by an American serviceman, was, according to the published recollections of Rifleman Alex Bowlby, considered risible by British front-line troops and fit only to be read out in a falsetto voice mimicking the affronted woman concerned. The Germans, however, clearly put faith in their concluding message: 'Would you still laugh if you considered that your sister, your girl or your wife at home might be the aim of the exploits by [sic] these "quick workers"? Obviously, the "blooming Americans" are much braver in England than at the front where you, poor devil, have got to fight German crack troops alone.'

*

Valerie Erskine Howe, for her part, had earlier let Anthony Ryshworth-Hill know of an approach made to her, writing in her typically droll and laconic fashion:

'An American said to me yesterday,
*   "I like your smile, come out with me?"*
*   "No."*
*   "No?"*
*   "No."*
*   "Are you married?"*
*   "No."*
*   "Engaged?"*
*   "No."*
*   "In love?"*
*   "Ha ha! – No. I'm not playing. Good-bye."*
*   "Good – what? Hey! Hi! Come back. Sa-ay . . .!"'*

Still, Valerie had conceded that *'from a purely physical point of view the American soldiers are better looking, i.e. more hygienic-looking than ours'*, and the clean-cut US serviceman certainly held an appeal for the likes of Heather Taylor, an English land girl. The Women's Land Army, first raised during the First World War to replace men who had left farm work to join the services, had been revived in 1939. Five years later, it numbered 80,000, with many Londoners, including Heather, from Streatham, among them. Her first placement, on a farm in Halesworth, Suffolk, was unhappy, the farmer's wife objecting to one of her boyfriends. Hearing of this, Heather's mother wrote on 7 October 1942 with words of advice,

misunderstanding the accusation levelled at her daughter that
she was 'dirty':

'... *Whatever has made the S[——]t family so vindictive? Of course,
I understand that country people are very conservative, and like no
ideas but their own, and I expect their ideas are about 25 years
behind London ones, and likely to remain there, but even so, what
was the trouble about Michael? So far as we know, you went to
some dances with him, which was quite an ordinary thing to do.
Was there anything else that the peculiar S[——]t mind could take
objection to? If so, you might tell us. As for you being dirty, do they
mean muddy? Because they knew before you went there that you
were going to work on the farm. Possibly she meant untidy, and if
she did (!) I can't answer for that one, but I can imagine.*'

Heather found Woodbridge, also in Suffolk, much more to her
taste. From August 1943, nearby Framlingham was home to the
US Army Air Force's 390th Bombardment Group, piloting B-17
Flying Fortresses on missions against German-occupied Europe.
Heather was able to indulge her love of dancing as a member of
the Framlingham Anglo-American Club where, from the evi-
dence of her photograph collection, she struck up a friendship
with one particular US airman called Rick, as well as with 'Sam
from Brooklyn'.

With such hospitable hosts living in such close proximity it
is not surprising that up to a quarter of the personnel serving at
American airbases in Britain during the Second World War took
British brides back to the United States. A friend of Heather's
sailed as one of 400 'GI Brides' aboard the US transport ship

Heather Taylor on a day out at Framlingham Castle with Rick.

Anglo-American Club,

FRAMLINGHAM.

This Ticket entitles the Holder to all Dances at above Club on payment of **9d.** for each Dance and must be **presented at the Door for inspection.**

Name MISS TAYLOR.

Until further notice Dances will be held every Tuesday evening from 7.45 to 11 p.m. and this is the only Notice Holders will receive.

If you leave the district you must not pass this card on to anyone else. Please return it to:—

MRS. J. POTTER,
Hon. Secretary
Ladies' Social Committee.

Heather's pass to the dances at the Anglo-American Club.

Bridgeport in January 1946, and subsequently wrote to her from Cleveland, Ohio.

Heather herself received a proposal – coincidentally also from Ohio – in December 1946, when an ex-serviceman known to us only as Rodney wrote her a letter quite startling in its intensity. First he asks her to imagine that he is in the room with her, rather than writing to her from across the Atlantic: '*In your own mind you must give me a body, you must give me warmth, lips, strong arms in which to hold you* . . .' He then goes on:

'*Can you remember the things you saw in me the night of our first meeting?* . . . *allow yourself the fantasy that I am standing in front of you now and saying these things that I am about to say* . . .

. . . I whisper that which I have never uttered until now. "I love you with all my heart and there will never be another" . . . *This is the message you have always wanted. It tells you that you are no longer alone. It tells you that you have a champion, that you have a strong man ready to lay the treasures of the earth and, more important, the treasures of his soul at your feet. He will love you, cherish you, honour you and fight for you all the days of his life* . . . *Are these not all the things a girl could want? You know that for this minute and for all time hence, you possess me and I possess you. We are inseparable. We are one* . . .

. . . Will you marry me and become my wife? Will you become as one with me for all the happy days of struggle and of pride, of personal victory and of loss, of warmth and happiness and of love abiding until the last breath . . .?

. . . I have always loved you from the time I first saw you . . . *nor will I ever stop loving you. Say that you love me and that you will*

be my bride ... I need you, Heather, as you need me. Have we not floated through life thus far, seeking, wanting, yearning? Have we both not been haunted through these months apart by the fond memory of one another? ... Are we not meant to be man and wife?

... This is only the start of happy days together. Days filled with love, adventure, travel, excitement ... I would die for you or live for you. I will spend my days in adoration at your shrine.

Do not wait to reply. Write to me now, for we both know of our love ... I insist that ... you and I were meant to be this way and I ... know that you will be my loving bride.

All my love to you, this day, and always,

Rodney.'

What made Rodney declare his passion so fervently after so many months when, by his own admission, he had never told her before that he loved her, we will never know; but we do know that in spite of his ardour Heather did not accept his proposal.

She never married.

ANTHONY UPFILL-BROWN

Anthony (Tony) Upfill-Brown, from Haywards Heath in Sussex, was an eighteen-year-old medical student at Cambridge when he was called up in 1942. He joined the Welsh Guards and was sent for basic training at the Guards Depot, Caterham. Although the same age as his contemporaries who had arrived there straight from school, Tony's year at university had left him more worldly-wise, something that his drill instructor, Sergeant Brassington, understood when imparting words of wisdom upon Tony's receipt of his first leave pass: '*Mr Upfill-Brown Sir, I imagine that you'll be looking for a bit of crumpet tonight. Take my advice, don't go for pretty young girls, go for their mums. They'll be bloody grateful.*'

Tony, in fact, recognized his own susceptibilities and later, in a last letter to his parents to be opened in the event of his death, admitted: '*the greatest worry I ever had is that there is too much*

of Grandpa Upfill in me, i.e. . . . women. I fall for every one I meet.'
And once he had gone through the Royal Military College,
Sandhurst, and been commissioned, the smart blue patrol jacket
and overalls (as opposed to khaki) worn by even a wartime
guards officer increased his allure to women. *'If I went out to
dinner in London, I'd wear blue. [That is] if I was taking some
young lady to the "Bag of Nails" or to some nasty night club at that
time, Coconut Grove or whatever it was, I would probably wear
blue – depending how important she was or I thought she was.'*

Upfill-Brown crossed to Normandy in June 1944 with the 2nd
Welsh Guards, part of the Guards Armoured Division, in the
immediate wake of D-Day, the Allied invasion of Nazi-occupied
Europe. Pummelled by superior British and American firepower,
German resistance in France had largely disintegrated by the end
of August and, heading into Belgium, the Welsh Guards were in
the forefront of the liberation of Brussels on 3 September. The
reception afforded the British by the people of the Belgian capital
was rapturous and Tony became particularly friendly with Lillian
Ritzer, who helped him improve his French beyond the *'Où est le
Bosch?'* (Where are the Germans?) of which it largely consisted.

Even when the Welsh Guards advanced beyond Brussels into
the Netherlands, Tony contrived to keep in touch with Lillian,
writing to his parents on 8 October: *'I got 24 hours' leave so set off
for Brussels. It's a hell of a way but it is well worth it. We had a great
time. I took the Blonde Lillian out to dinner but there wasn't time
to go to a nightclub as there is a curfew at 12 for everyone. The next
morning I went shopping. Got myself a pipe as Lillian insisted on
giving me one.'*

Tony with Lillian Ritzer (right) and her sister Edith.

Tony's parents, however, were more concerned about their son's liaison with his cousin Avril, who was in the Women's Auxiliary Air Force; they appear to have worried that he was toying with her affections. Tony was contrite: *'I quite agree with you about everything you say about Avril. And how right you are about me. I realize a lot of the time that I am "in love with love" as you put it. I haven't really been in love with anybody in my life, except perhaps myself – which is bad! And for a while with Rosemary, the girl you met at Cambridge, but that was more of an experiment than anything else. Anyway it taught me a hell of a lot . . . .'*

A few weeks later, however, Tony had a new enthusiasm in view: a childhood friend had appeared on the scene. He wrote to his parents on 28 November: *'By the way, of utmost importance. I have heard Ruth Barton is in Brussels. For heaven's sake find out her address and let me have it. I am due to go there again soon. And to be able to speak to a girl who actually talks English. My my! It seems unbelievable to me that girls do speak English. Do remember as soon as possible . . .'*

Ruth Barton worked for the Foreign Office and her arrival spelt the end for Lillian *'who,'* Tony later wistfully recalled, *'I rather deserted when Ruth came along, which I've always regretted.'*

Tony lost no time in taking Ruth out to dinner. He wrote that they had champagne, a 1934 Veuve Clicquot costing 1500 francs, *'which is cheap for Brussels'*. They went on to a nightclub, which closed at 11 p.m., *'so we went to a bottle party where we danced all the time. If H[aywards] H[eath] could have seen us – we were the only English couple in Brussels I should think and I hope kept up the British tradition.'*

The cheapness of champagne was none the less relative, and Tony closed his letter with a request: *'Now listen carefully, Ma. Will you enclose a £1 postal order in each letter you write me, so that I can have some money when I go to Brussels. My pay doesn't do much good.'*

The next time he was able to get to Brussels to meet Ruth was 3 January 1945. Again they went out and danced into the small hours, Tony getting back to his unit *'in time (just) for 1st parade of the day'*. He told his mother: *'it is heaven having Ruth in B[russels] because we both get homesick together and gossip about all the people we know. We discovered last night that Ruth had a pash on me when I was 12. And I had one on her when I was 16 . . . I hope to be able to get there again sometime next week. It makes a wonderful change and raises my morale considerably. Also she is rather sweet. So now you see why I want those postal orders!'*

Writing to his sister Jill a fortnight later, Tony's account of the high jinks indulged in by Ruth and himself was slightly racier: *'I went into Brussels last night to take Ruth out to dinner . . . Had lots of champagne so we were quite happy. She is most amusing, I haven't laughed so much for ages. Everyone thinks she is Belgian, until she speaks, so they talk to me as if she wasn't there. As you can imagine, they say some pretty low things, i.e. "are you going to be sleeping with her tonight?" She takes it very well and laughs like a drain!'*

Ruth was popular, and Tony was well aware that she had to be shared:

' . . . the other night I was . . . having tea with R. when one of her boyfriends rolled up. I am always pulling her leg about how she keeps on getting two people wanting to take her out on the same night. She is good about it actually, she never breaks a date; at least she hasn't ever done so with me. So I did a big act and told her to go off with the boyfriend – clever I thought – good type, don't ye know! Anyway, gave me a good excuse to go out on a party! Trouble was, ended up very high at the same night club – most amusing! Still as every one else was high it didn't matter much!'

While Tony could play the 'good type' in public, privately he was torn. At a party on 30 January Ruth, as he noted in his

Tony Upfill-Brown (far right) and his tank, Brussels, September 1944.

diary, had been 'very sweet, indeed *tres* sentimental'. Yet, there again, he knew that the two of them were living in a highly artificial situation and the war must resume in the spring, with the Western Allies and Soviets pushing on into the German heartlands: '*I suppose I am wasting my time taking out an English girl in B[russels]*', he wrote home, '*but we do have fun. Anyway I should think the circumstance we are in at the moment won't last much longer, we'll have to back up the Russians a bit.*'

Meanwhile Avril, having not heard from Tony regularly enough for her taste, had taken small revenge, leaving him to complain to his parents: '*I haven't heard from that damn girl Av for about two weeks, so I don't know what she is up to now!!*' News from Brussels, however, had a galvanizing effect, as he crowed a month later: *'Avril excelled herself. I got 3 letters running over my birthday. Between you and me, I think I made her jealous by telling her about Ruth . . .'*

In March 1945 the 2nd Welsh Guards became engaged in the Rhineland battles in earnest. The ferocity of the fighting for the Wesel bridgehead left Tony philosophical and made him forthcoming about where he stood with the women in his life.

'By the way, you mustn't worry about me ever marrying Av. I had just written to tell her that I had no intention of doing same. But for all that, I am still very fond of the old thing. I like her more than the others I know. But I must admit I am getting a very soft spot for Ruth. We are just great friends and have every intention of keeping it that way. I reckon friendships with girls can go 3 ways. 1) you remain friends. 2) you get too friendly, which leads to two things: 3) Marriage. Or kissing and petting which doesn't do either of you any good, and if you carry that to its natural conclusion then there are lots of tears and people hurt. Dog's life.'

Tony had reached a state of equilibrium. His unit was across the Rhine and advancing rapidly. He was looking forward to some home leave on 17 April. Then, on 7 April, near Lengerich during the Welsh Guards' drive on Bremen, catastrophe struck. A German self-propelled gun sent an armour-piercing shell through the turret of his Cromwell tank. Tony's left leg and much of his right were carried away. Evacuated back to hospital in Brussels, Tony received a visitor: *'Ruth came in this morning to see me, bless her. She is in splendid form. Sweet of her to write to Ma.*

She is a honey.' A long convalescence followed in England. Without this life-changing event, Tony admitted, he would probably have married Avril after all.

As it was, he married Jennifer, the young ward of the surgeon who operated on him.

CECIL MAY

Cecil May, a soldier in his mid-thirties, crossed to France as a member of the Royal Army Service Corps on 27 June 1944. His wartime diaries suggest that his chief purpose in life was attending dances and the pursuit of women and, having cut something of a swathe across blackout Britain, his transfer to the Continent simply presented him with fresh opportunities. His necessarily abbreviated accounts of his adventures provide an instructive insight into the life of a fancy-free soldier abroad.

From 20 October onwards Cecil's unit was stationed at Ostend. On Saturday 18 November he went to a dance in a local café: *'Packed and only a small place. Met two girls. Frank and I took them home. Mine's a little blonde called Betty . . .'*

Cecil arranged to meet 22-year-old Betty, from Westende, eight miles down the coast, the very next day. *'Worked till 5.30 . . .*

then went round to meet the two girls [who] took us home to Betty's place. Very clean, but I think they are poor.' Belgium had only recently been liberated, and indulging in romantic entanglements with the locals carried the risk of inheriting a girlfriend from the German *Wehrmacht. 'Betty during the German Occupation worked in a photographers. Showed us lots of snaps taken by the Germans. Think she must have been with a few of the Bosch though she denied it. Seems a nice innocent kid.'*

Over the next two days he received disquieting news: *'Heard that Betty is a collaborator and knocked about with the Bosch, and that her brother bunked with the Germans.'* Further confirmation followed when his friend Frank told Cecil that Betty had been imprisoned by former resistance fighters and made to scrub out

As British soldiers look on, a female collaborator in the Pas de Calais is marched away by members of the Resistance.

the barracks, and that her brother would be shot if he was caught.

None of this deterred him, however, and on Monday 27 November he wrote: *'Finished work at 9.00. Went straight round Betty's. She mended my coat sleeve for me. We had a kiss and cuddle. She told me she was in the family way by a Jerry. Was pulling my leg I think (I hope!). Said afterwards she was joking!'*

Sometimes news of the war intruded. On 19 December he wrote in his diary: *'Ardennes offensive. Rumours that the Jerries have got a bashing, like the Falaise Gap. Anyway tons of bombers came over. Machine gunning at Ostende in the streets. And four soldiers found stabbed in the back at Bruges.'*

On Christmas Eve, Cecil had some bad news for Betty. His unit was being moved to Bruges, over twenty miles from Westende, making it more difficult for him to see her. *'She cried and said it was better if she had never met me. Cold in her house so got on the couch and put my coat over us. Had quite a good time. Think she is fond of me. Gave me a photo of herself. Stayed till 11.20 . . .'*

The same train of events was played out three days later: *'. . . went round to Betty's. She cried and said her mother was dying and she would be all alone. Managed to cheer her up a bit . . . Felt very miserable.'*

Once at Bruges, Cecil was reflective. *'Still feel fed up leaving Betty, one of the best girls I've met . . . Was tempted to tell her I would marry her but thought it well over and decided not.'* In a letter to his mother, he wrote: *'Now don't start thinking I am going to bring a Belgian wife home or something . . . the Belgians are not as*

Cecil May.

good looking as the English girls, but this one was better ... I used to laugh at her. Sometimes [when] she couldn't quite understand what I meant she used to stamp her feet. But she soon forgot and was nearly always smiling. I miss her at this place.'

Well might he miss her. The pickings in Bruges were meagre: at the Minerva Dance Hall there were three soldiers to every girl: *'Couldn't fix up with any girl to take home. They seem windy of the British soldier ... A lot of them go home to bed at 9.00 or 10.00. They are so used to going to bed because of no coal and sometimes no light that they always do it. Plus I think there's quite a lot of Pro-Nazis here. Tried a turn with another girl ... she has a sergeant here and he wasn't there last night but she wouldn't play. Saucy little dame though. Wish my Betty was here.'*

Cecil attempted to keep Betty in play, but a long-distance relationship in wartime was hard work. On four occasions she was not at home when he called and he had a wasted journey. His visit on 17 January 1945 was one of the more successful:

'Had my ½ day finished by 12.30. Hitch-hiked to Weste-End-Bael. Had a job: had 4 lifts, got there by 4.00. Gave Betty some soup and chocolate. Her mother was sitting in the chair with a blanket round her. [She] looks ill, I think she won't last long. Betty pleased to see me. Had some tea there, cold herrings and coffee and brown bread. Never ate much as they have very little food, [they] save it for the brother who is in prison I think. The mother started to cry when I asked about him. She forgets perhaps he's killed other lads and made mothers cry. I think he fought with the Germans but am not sure. Had a kiss and a cuddle after the mother went to bed.'

At the end of March, Cecil was posted to Brussels. His romance with Betty had run its course. A visit to the Belgian capital two months earlier when on leave had already alerted him to the potential of his new hunting ground:

'... *went to the 21 Club to a dance packed with soldiers. Picked up a nice little medical student of 17½! But she would not let me take her home ... Before that went in the Montgomery Club for tea. Saw a smashing little dark-haired waitress there, tried to make a date but she worked till 9.30 and was too tired. Said she would meet me the next week as she finished at 2.00 in the afternoon* [but as he lamented in a letter to his mother: *'Am afraid I shan't be there though! Still she was very nice and understood my bad*

The Montgomery Club for British servicemen was operated by the Navy,
Army and Air Force Institutes (NAAFI) and opened in 1944.

Cecil described the Montgomery Club waitresses as 'smashing'.

French!'] ... Left the dance at 10.30, had a walk round La Gare du Nord and went in some of the brothels. Were the women rough, phew, blokes were paying 700 Francs and they were old bags. Tried to get me and Arthur and Reg upstairs but we would not wear it. Bought them some wine and had a laugh and that's all.'

So it was that by August 1945, having fully got the measure of Brussels, Cecil entertained hopes of a blonde dressmaker called Mariette: *'Finished at 5.30 and went round to the Baudwin* [Baudouin Club]. *Getting on quite well with the Blonde. But so far haven't had a chance to take her out and try her technique!*

Her father and mother were there. Come especially to look me over I suppose . . .'

At first he found her rather frustratingly prim. *'Had a date with Mariette . . . at 4 o'clock in front of the Palace Hotel . . . Took her home and she said goodbye right in front of a café and wouldn't let me kiss her goodnight! Rather like her but don't seem to get far . . . [she] seems scared of the soldiers . . .'* He hoped to impress her by taking her to a dance at the Théâtre Royal de la Monnaie, popularly known to the British as the Money Exchange, the home of the National Opera and one of the most glamorous venues in the city. His diary entry for the evening is particularly vivid:

'All the posh of Brussels was there, evening dress . . . 150 francs just to dance and the first balcony 1000 francs and so on. The theatre is very much like Covent Garden Opera House, only not so big. Three bands. Just before 12.00 there was a Victory Parade which included a contingent of Coldstream Guards, Yankee Airborne and Free French and some Belgian Regulars. The Guards were the first in Brussels. The Airborne Yanks fought in the Ardennes. Came in through a door and down some steps to the sound of the bagpipes. The Guards were first and they were easily the best of the bunch. Made you proud to be an Englishman. They were head and shoulders taller than the rest and their halt was with one "Bang" that shook the building. The Belge weren't too bad. The Yanks sloppy as per. And the bagpipes were grand, and the drummers. Quite enjoyed the show, but for dancing [it] was far too packed and hot . . . Took Mariette home. Left her place after a bit of necking. She's getting better! And had to walk the whole way from Searbeek

Saturday night in Brussels, 1945. One of Cecil's diary entries reads: 'Went to a dance Sat. But it was so packed you could hardly move . . .'

to G. de Nord. Then to Port de Ninove and then to Dilbeek and not a waggon passed me till right outside the billets. Got in OK at 4.00 and wasn't missed.'

Before long, however, Cecil began to suspect that all was not well with their relationship: *'Rode my Bike to Mariette's place . . . Mariette not there. She had gone out shopping with a married woman called Josey and didn't come [home] till 9.00. Felt a bit wild after me getting there. Monday night she and Josey went dancing in a café and I think they were with some Yank officer who bought champagne for them. Think I'm wasting my time there.'*

Matters reached a head on Saturday 22 September when

Mariette told Cecil she could not come out the following night because she had to finish making a coat. *'Am a bit suspicious that she has another date,'* he wrote. On Sunday, Cecil went out alone, only to make a discovery which, while unwelcome, could not have come as a surprise:

'Went into the 21 Club … caught sight of Mariette there. [She] took no notice till I bumped right into her, and was I mad! … I told her she was a liar, and didn't have the courage to tell me she was coming here, and finished up with "Vous dit s'marines!" [Tell it to the Marines, the classic expression of disbelief] *… She got wild as well but talked so fast that I didn't understand her. Shoved her, I wasn't standing any messing about!'*

The 21 Club where Cecil had his break-up with Mariette.

Cecil remained in Brussels until he was demobilized in March 1946. The months since his break-up with Mariette had not been lonely: Loulou, Anny and Irina, a Polish nurse, all pass through the pages of his diary. But although Cecil had, at the time, longed to return home and berated the new Labour Government for not arranging it sooner, ironically the last entry in his diary, in 1947, was to convey the plaintive quality of a lament: *'Am cheesed off. Civvy street is too unexciting and dull. Would like to be back in Bruxelles with some of the boys.'*

Truly, the grass is always greener . . .

JOHN RHODES AND
JOAN PENDLEBURY

Lance-Corporal John Rhodes, a lawyer by profession, had been sent out to India in 1941 to join the 3rd Carabiniers, a British cavalry regiment which had only undergone mechanization four years before. He left behind in Blackpool the object of his devotion, Joan Pendlebury, a friend of the family whom he addressed fondly in a letter sent to his parents from Karachi on 11 December 1941: *'To "Our" Joan – in answer to your question in your letter written on holiday – I'm still smiling – I always will be now ... The words I said when I said goodbye are perhaps if possible more true now than they were even then. I love you – need I say more?'*

John's regiment, having been re-equipped with American Grant and Lee tanks and trained in their use, was committed to action in 1944 with the 14th Army in Burma. In April and May the 3rd Carabiniers were heavily engaged during the Battle of Imphal, a successful defensive action which prevented the Japanese breaking through into India. Fought in conjunction with the equally decisive Battle of Kohima, Imphal-Kohima had by July cost the enemy over 50,000 of the 85,000 troops they brought to the field. The 3rd Carabiniers afterwards joined in the 14th Army's drive south into Burma in pursuit of the retreating Japanese and, when John wrote to Joan on 3 December, the regiment was preparing to cross the River Chindwin. In his letter John expressed anxiety, not at the prospect of action, but because a previous letter of his had upset Joan, a not uncommon misunderstanding when a couple, separated by thousands of miles, were only able to communicate irregularly and sentiment was difficult to express.

'Dearest Joan,

I've just received your Air Mail Letter Card written after receiving that utterly foolish letter of mine. I've written an Air Mail Letter in reply at some length but am writing this too in case it should reach you quicker. I cannot very well cable from here. I'm terribly sorry about that letter I wrote – when I received your reply I assure you the realization that I had hurt you of all people was even more painful to me than the receiving by you of that letter. You see, really and truly, I love you, I always will, my memories haven't changed, my ideals haven't changed, my thoughts of you haven't changed and I'm thinking of you always . . . I'm hoping to be at any rate on my way home within another six months or so and I want to see you so much. Will you let me know your address from time to time so *that I can cable to you immediately I dock and I may be able to call to see you on my way home. I hope with all my heart you will have a really good and happy Christmas with everything you desire – somewhere at the back of beyond I'll be thinking of you and say a little prayer just for you – just as I did with a lighted candle in a little Church in other mountains years ago . . .'*

John clearly felt able to confide his innermost feelings to Joan, writing: *'The going has been pretty tough but I'm still smiling through . . . I'm tired Joan – utterly tired of it all . . . I could have made things much more easy for myself if I'd taken the easy way, but I wanted to march and fight and be with the fittest and the best. I have no regrets – I would still rather have it like that, come what may . . . I'm trying to climb a mountain to an ideal . . .'*

He wrote again on 9 December: *'I've been terribly worried since I wrote that stupid letter to you but am happy now because I feel sure all is well with us.'* He was concerned that Joan, a corporal in the Auxiliary Territorial Service, should not have financial worries; women in the ATS were paid only two-thirds the rate of a serving soldier. *'You must not go short of anything while you are in the services and particularly must never be short of money to enable you to obtain anything you need – it is now difficult at any time for me to send you anything from here, and at present of course it is impossible, but if now or at any time in the future you need anything for any reason do let me know and you know I will make the necessary arrangements . . .'*

He told her that she was his inspiration, and that she gave him both comfort and courage: *'I love you so much Joan – throughout my army life I've been classified as an A1 man and a*

John Rhodes.

first line combatant – that's as I wanted it to be – I wanted it that way because I believed in my heart that anything less than the best was not good enough for you – I'm not a strong man or a particularly brave one but I've always been with the toughest and the best and by the Grace of God remain there – I trust I always will – it's been that way because I believed you would prefer it that way – and because of you through all the years – through the initial humiliation – through the tough going and all the hazards – I've made the grade – made it because I thought of you and because of you had the strength to go on.

In latter years we have had a youngster with us – a youngster very much in love with his girl called Elsie – and believe it or not when the going's tough out of the wallet in his pocket comes his photograph of Elsie – and he carries on. The same applies to me but my picture of Joan is in my mind and always in my heart . . .'

Although, as the war progressed, communication between distant theatres of fighting and home had improved, John for one still felt deprived if a month elapsed and he had not heard from Joan. On 16 December, he wrote: *'I received your letter of 1 December today. The last one I received was 18 November and it seems ages since I got that one so I think some must have gone astray somewhere – but such is life. It may well be that I shall be unable to write for a little while but I know you will understand – shall write just as soon and as often as I possibly can.'*

He was thoroughly weary of war, and grateful that Joan appreciated what he was going through: *I'm more than inclined to agree with you that 3 years of this is enough for any man – and maybe after 3 years and 4 months of it I should know – and quite certainly over a year up here mostly in action is in the nature of what one might call a belly full.'*

His main preoccupation at this time was to reassure her that he would come back to her: '*I had a photograph of my little niece the other day – she is very beautiful – one day perhaps she will be as beautiful as my Joan – I am resolved that she will never need to be ashamed of Uncle John. And believe me I shall come back – so long as you are free and I know I can return and you will be there just as I left you. I shall return come hell or high water Joan one day I shall come back to you.*' He wrote her a deeply heartfelt plea that she should wait for him, quoting (and occasionally misquoting) lines from a poem by Russian war correspondent Konstantin Simonov, called, appropriately, 'Wait For Me'.

'*Wait for me – I will come back. Only wait – and wait. Wait though rainclouds louring black make you desolate. Wait though winter snowstorms whirl, wait though summer's hot. Wait though no one else will wait . . . Wait though from the distant front not one letter comes; Wait though everyone who waits sick of it becomes. Wait for me – I will come back. Pay no heed to those who'll so glibly tell you that it is vain to wait. Though my friends abandon hope and back there at home rise and toast my memory wrapped in silence pained, Wait. And when they drink that toast leave your glass undrained. Wait for me – I will come back, though from Death's own jaws. Let the friends who did not wait think it chance, no more. They will never understand, those who did not wait how it was YOUR waiting that saved me in the war. And the reason I've come through we shall know, we two: simply this, you waited as no one else could do.*'

John's letters were, in the main, earnest affairs and not much given to levity. Mentioning Joan's existence to his fellow soldiers out in Burma, however, gave rise to some inevitable ribbing which he felt sufficiently sure of himself to relay:

'As a matter of interest the blokes around here (they're a pretty terrible lot sometimes with a somewhat ribald sense of humour) keep impressing the fact on me that a W[ar] S[ubstantive] Corporal in the ATS can only be stripped [of her rank] *by Court Martial and they keep asking me what I'm going to do about it – being a bit dumb the penny hasn't dropped yet – I keep telling 'em that if I have you court martialled you'll lose your pay and we can't afford that – maybe I'd have to go out to work.'*

When John wrote to Joan on 13 February 1945, a harder tone crept into his letter. He had begun by discussing his prospects once the war had ended. He would return to his law firm and provide for his mother, who had recently been widowed. But in expressing the hope that he and Joan might marry, John drew her attention to the unedifying choices facing him if she did not, implicitly inviting her to rescue him from the prospect of a loveless marriage to another or empty womanizing.

'I've also to decide I suppose whether to marry or not. That depends to a large extent on you. If you and I were to marry, which is one of those things which at present is problematical, I should naturally expend the whole of my energy, resources and such talent as I have in building a real home and family, and making the office into something big and substantial to support and serve the welfare of

An American M3 General Lee Medium Tank of the type driven
by John Rhodes' unit, Burma 1944.

*home and family . . . and to ensure the future of those who follow
and give them better opportunities and a fuller and more pleas-
urable life. If I were to do all that I should marry for love –
meaning I should marry you. If I don't or you don't another problem confronts me – should I marry for social reasons and for a
future home or remain a bachelor. I don't know – frankly in all
probability in the absence of a marriage for love at my stage I
should doubtless remain a bachelor and to put it perhaps a little
crudely have a woman as and when it was necessary and for so long
as it was necessary or convenient. It is probably a certainty I shall
remain a bachelor. That is likely to alter my views about a lot of
things – women in particular – and as to what I do about that –
since to some bachelors they are as necessary at times as to any other*

man – I shall consider nobody's business, please myself and tell the critics whoever they may be to go to hell.

Certainly if I don't marry I don't propose to work very hard since with what I have and with what I can earn in comfort it won't be necessary [to do so] to support merely myself and my periodical whims and fancies. If it should work out like that I'll probably spend most of my time away on some mad scheme, travel or adventure, but I assure you I shan't join the Army again – in fact after this shambles I wouldn't join a goddam Christmas Club.'

He asked her to think about it: *'. . .particularly I'd like your views on the subject . . .'* and made it plain what she might be letting herself in for:

'Four years abroad has not improved my patience or my temper and I've always been blessed with little of the former and a lot of the latter. When I get back I don't intend to go to sleep – I intend to make things move and make them move quick . . . One minor detail is that I've been deprived of female company for a long time – something which is and always has been unnatural to me – when it's presented to me again in unlimited quantities and with unlimited opportunities I'm afraid it will be necessary for me to act quickly before something untowards happens – there are only three things to do – marry for love, marry for social reasons and a home or remain a bachelor and acquire a female to alleviate the urge for the rest. You may not understand all this but maybe you will.'

And then, in the second half of February, just as the 14th Army was preparing for the next big river crossing, the Irrawaddy, news came through that 115 rank and file of the 3rd Carabiniers, having served up to four years overseas, were eligible for repatriation to the United Kingdom, John among them. The repercussions for the regiment, about to embark on four months' hard fighting which would see the British push through all the way to the Burmese capital Rangoon, were highly destabilizing, the Carabiniers' war diary reporting 'chaos in Squadrons regarding replacement of tried and blooded crews'; but for John all that mattered was that he would soon see Joan again: '...*something I have been waiting for a very long time has really come true at last – I am so happy that I'm even daring to hope you have been waiting through the years for the same thing.*'

The prospect of his return, however, made his need for certainty all the more urgent: '*I have decisions to make now and a new life to build and on those decisions will depend what kind of a life it is going to be.*' On 23 February he wrote expressing a combination of hope and resignation. The letter is disarming in its honesty:

'*I don't know how you and I will fare on reunion Joan – I wouldn't like to hazard a guess – manlike I suppose I'll want to go on from where I left off – there have been so many changes since then that will be hardly likely or possible and since I've been unnaturally suppressed for so long I'm likely to be a little stupid and inclined to bungle things ... I'm afraid there is little of anything to tell ... I've eaten plenty and slept plenty and washed plenty and that's always good for a man, and the relief from nervous and mental strain and tension is better. I've done practically all my shopping and I'm all set and raring to go. I want to see you so much if only for a little while … my soldiering days of course are not over … it may be hello and goodbye again – or it may not be – we shall see – in any event I am not afeared. I wanted to marry you but that will probably not be possible – for the present to see you once again will suffice – after seeing you I must and will know once and for all. In any event we'll have a good time, the best and happiest even – and after that – well – no doubt the lady will have to decide. They tell me I'm still mad as ever so there should never be a dull moment. I love you – too much. Had I loved you less doubtless – womanlike – you would have loved me more. God bless and keep you … just as I promised – I will come back. All my love as always.'*

John returned home and was demobilized from the army in December 1945. Did he and Joan get married?

The answer is yes.

Nigel Gunnis

Major Nigel Gunnis, commissioned into the Territorial Army in 1938, was a socially well-connected officer with a Heavy Anti-Aircraft Regiment of the Royal Artillery. By 1944 he was finalizing a divorce and his chief correspondent while serving abroad – first in Tunisia and then Italy – was his mother. Nigel wrote to let her know that even on active service he could maintain a social life. *'I can't remember if I told you about the dance. It was very grand, about four hundred people there and lots of American nurses in evening dress. Our own poor nurses in their rather severe uniforms found it rather unfair competition. I took two from my friendly hospital who thoroughly enjoyed it I think. Anyway it didn't end till after 2 a.m. They ran it rather on the lines of a hunt ball, tickets at 15/–* [fifteen shillings] *and supper and drinks thrown in.'*

The report of his activities on 10 June 1944 was less satisfactory: '*The Colonel and I took out two dreadful American women last week. His idea not mine! A bad evening, as one got very tiddly!*' The following month, however, he had escorts of whose backgrounds he could be sure. '*I went to a dance the other night with the Red Cross where I have two old friends, one Dorothy Meynell whose father was at Eton with me and the other Gypsy Lawrence whose brother was at Cambridge with me. Quite a good party.*'

Quite why, in the autumn of 1944, Nigel was then chosen to be part of the British Military Mission to Romania, is uncertain. Perhaps it was because his brother, Rupert, a well-known Hellenist and art lover, knew the country. Nigel himself was well travelled.

Romania, having seen its armies heavily defeated by the forces of Britain and America's ally the Soviet Union, had recently changed sides in the war and was now fighting against the Germans. Although Winston Churchill, in a meeting with the Soviet leader Joseph Stalin in Moscow in October 1944, had thrashed out an agreement concerning the degree of Soviet – as opposed to British and American – influence in Balkan countries soon to be liberated from the Germans, the proportion in Romania (where the Soviet Red Army was already present) was settled at 90 per cent to 10 per cent in the Soviets' favour. The British contribution to the Allied Control Commission in Romania was never going to have much clout, and Nigel would have to find other means of keeping himself busy. Still, he had at least been issued the official guide for British servicemen posted to Romania which, regarding women, carried the following advice:

'The Roumanian attitude towards women is very different from our own. Roumanian girls of the middle class are very strictly looked after until their marriage, which is generally a business arrangement. It is, therefore, most unusual for an unmarried girl to accept invitations from a man. On the other hand, the morals of Roumanian married women, many of whose husbands are considerably older than themselves, are often elastic.'

In December, a month after arriving in the Romanian capital, Bucharest, Nigel informed his mother that life was proving not intolerable. *'The Colonel and I are having a party tonight in our house. About thirty people coming. All very mixed: Russians, Americans, Roumanians, etc., but it should be quite good as we've wonderful things to eat and drink and have a gypsy band and the best known singer in Roumania to entertain. My bedroom will as usual be the dance floor! So heaven knows when I shall get to bed!'*

Nigel had assistance in his party-planning; the appeal of well-to-do British army officers (even ones who were nearing forty) to Romanian womenfolk was evidently great: *'The "girl friends" have been very good about keeping us and lent us plates etc. . . . The Colonel and I have got some charming "pin up girls" who help us with our parties and generally more or less run the house and do odd shopping for us! They are really very nice people here and we've made some good friends – it's a pity that times are not more settled as they've nearly all got places in the country and on Sinaia and other places which I believe are charming, but due to one thing and another they can't get there now – and so we can't see them.'*

The women who featured chiefly in Nigel's social life were

Nigel and Suzanne at Constanza.

Colette, Suzanne, Anca Popp, known to all as Popp, and, confusingly, Popette, whom Nigel called Poppet. On 31 December they helped him to see in the new year in traditional fashion: '*Had a good party on New Years Eve and got home at 6.30 next morning. Had to be in the office by 9 so I didn't get much sleep! It was a very gay party though, about eighty people in one of my girl friends' houses, all young things! We all paid our share and had masses to eat and drink. Plenty of Champagne – Roumanian, but it's not bad.*'

Nigel's circle of female acquaintances, and party-going generally, kept him occupied in February 1945. '*I went and saw some very good Roumanian dancing yesterday afternoon (Sunday) all in their national costumes. It's extraordinary how much they love dancing and all the girls whom one meets socially know the national dances, which are very complicated. Quite a few of my friends were dancing yesterday. After, I took my girl friend out to dinner at quite an amusing little restaurant. Good food and a band.'*

Yet even such levels of conviviality were to prove as nothing compared to the big event of the following month:

'I had a tremendous birthday! In the evening Colette – No.1 Girlfriend – gave a party for me in her house. A great success. About twenty of my best friends and lots of good things to eat. There was a special cake which I had to cut, and champagne. I can't remember when I had such a birthday, or am likely to have such another. They really were all very sweet to me and are so natural and friendly, although they are all half my age! But they marry so dreadfully young that they have all been married about five years and so seem much older than they really are. I've just been speaking to Colette on the telephone and told her how I was writing to you about her party. She was thrilled! One wonders though what the future holds for them all.'

The onset of summer saw the end of the war in Europe. Although tensions between the Western Allies and the Soviets would soon precipitate the Cold War, for Nigel the balmy days of June 1945 meant that he could entertain his girlfriends at the country retreat he and two other British officers had rented for themselves. He had invested too in a couple of cameras and sent his mother some contact prints of photographs capturing the occasion: *'I thought the enclosed photographs would amuse you. You will need a magnifying glass to see them. They are taken with*

Sonia, Anca Popp and Colette, Snagov.

my camera at my Villa in Snagov – I've written who's who on the back. Popp and Colette are my great friends, the latter particularly, and they are the ones who gave me my birthday party and everything. They come down to the Villa nearly every weekend . . . It's a complete picnic, but the greatest fun.'

At Snagov, half an hour from Bucharest, Nigel also socialized with the young King Michael of Romania, whose bold arrest of the dictator Marshal Ion Antonescu the previous August had ended the country's alliance with Germany.

'The King took me out in his speed boat last time I was there which was rather fun and we tore up and down the lake at about 50 m.p.h. He's like a schoolboy and delighted in going as close as he could to rowing boats and . . . making them rock about. However

Nigel (right) and HM King Michael (left, driving boat) at Snagov.

all the people are very fond of him and didn't seem to mind! Last weekend I went to Colette's vineyard about thirty miles away (I've sent you photographs of my girl friends so I hope you will now know who I am talking about!). It was very interesting and an amusing weekend. We tasted so many different wines that after lunch on Sunday I fell into a semi intoxicated stupor. I must say so did everyone else. So I did not let down British prestige!'

By now Nigel's mother, apprised of his jaunts, was moved to ask a rather obvious question. Nigel, in his response, laughed it off: '*You ask about Colette's husband. Oh, yes, there is one. Very nice, and we're great friends. Thank heavens, though, he doesn't always come!*'

Nor was it just Nigel who found Romanian women pleasing

262

Nigel and Colette.

company. His fellow officers were equally enraptured, as Nigel confirmed in a letter of 27 September 1945:

'I'm very busy at the moment trying to arrange for about half the Mission to get married. Well when I say half the Mission, I've got about twelve on my books at the moment. I suppose I shall have to act as chief sponsor or something. I'm going to have them all done at the same time I think. What a party that will be! There are so many complications too, but I suppose like many others we shall get over them and a good time will be had by all, excluding me. If only I could write the inner history of the British Mission to Roumania it would make an amusing book, but alas would never pass the censor!'

So well were the existing members of the Mission suited that Nigel, writing home the following month, had fears for new

One of the many weddings which Nigel helped to organize between British officers and Romanian women.

arrivals: *'Today the long awaited and for my part, as I shall have to look after them, "long-dreaded" ATS* [the women of the Auxiliary Territorial Service] *arrived. One officer and three girls. All have faces like boots and I fear are going to find life rather dull, as all members of this Mission have their own friends now and I cannot see that these girls will get taken out much!'*

By February 1946, Nigel's family and his girlfriends were sending each other presents, as one of his letters to his mother makes evident. *'I'm sorry you had to bury Colette's paté, I won't say anything, as she took so much trouble about making it. I see her and Poppet more or less daily; they are both very well and send you messages. They keep on saying that they are going to write to you, but won't do so till I help!'*

There follows an insertion in Popette's handwriting:

'Here I am at last! Forgive me for not having written you before to thank so much for the nice belt. I shall wear it on my white dresses in summer.

I have seen the photographs of you which Nigel took when he was at home. I think he resembles you very much. We have seen him in civilian clothes for the first time and found he is very "chic".

Inea is delighted with the nice bib that Diana [Nigel's daughter] *made for her, and Alina is very proud of her apron. I think they are very nicely made. Now I must stop other there will not be any room left for Nigel. Again many thanks, with love from Popette.'*

Nigel resumes:

'I am lunching here today, hence the above!
   Very best love,
   Loving Nigel'

While the homely nature of such correspondence might suggest that Nigel's liaisons with his Romanian girlfriends were innocent, there is no denying that the relationships contained a flirtatious element. After his return to England in 1947, and before the Communist coup that saw King Michael deposed, another of his friends, Sonia, wrote Nigel a letter full of catty gossip, recollected his penchant for slim women, and addressed him variously as 'Nigy', 'Nigelica' and ... 'Nigelicious'!

It is perhaps not surprising that when Nigel remarried in 1948, his new wife ensured that he had nothing more to do with his Romanian girlfriends.

ALAN AND JOY GLENDINNING

Alan Glendinning, a qualified doctor, had joined the Indian Medical Service in 1937, aged thirty-one. Caught up in the fall of Singapore in February 1942, he had endured three and a half years of captivity at the hands of the Japanese before the dropping of the atomic bombs on Hiroshima and Nagasaki in August 1945 brought an end to the war in the East. Alan had been held throughout as a prisoner of war at Changi Gaol on Singapore Island and was formally liberated when the 5th Indian Division arrived by sea on 5 September. The small Recovery of Allied Prisoners of War and Internees Control Team (RAPWI) which accompanied the 5th Division swung into action with impressive speed – even though on arrival it had discovered 37,000 prisoners of war in Singapore rather than the 10,000 it had expected – and within the following three weeks nearly all were evacuated, the sickest of them by air. A day after liberation, Alan took the opportunity to write to his wife, Joy, using a variety of pet names ('Sunny' and 'Sebastian'). Years apart had made Alan envisage their reunion very precisely.

'Hello, Little Sun,

It is quite hopeless at a time like this to give you any sort of idea of what I have been doing all these years. I can tell you that I am very well and, as far as I can judge myself, not altered in any way. I am working as hard as I have ever done in my life and have been all the way through, except when I have been sick myself and taken a busman's holiday in the hospital. As you can guess everything is chaotic here, and I am trying to write this letter with about as much peace and quiet as I would have in the middle of Euston Station. I want to tell you all the personal things I used to write but find it mighty hard. For years, like everybody else, I have been keeping my emotions locked up and simply not using them, and now when I am suddenly able to let go a bit I hardly know where or how to start. But for me you are still everything in the world, and everything I understand in the way of freedom, and happiness and fun. Every single day since I left you I have thought and remembered and looked forward. And now to my absolute astonishment it looks as if I might be with you in a very few weeks. None of us can really believe it, but now when we are beginning to see faces from outside it is gradually sinking in.

The absolute essential is that we should have some days to ourselves to begin with, and I have been thinking that London will be the best place for you to meet me. Will you do what you can to make advance bookings, if possible in the Cumberland Hotel, and then when I can advise you about when I am likely to arrive you can pop over and get yourself established. I can hardly believe that I am really writing those sorts of instructions and advises even now. I have thought of them so often, and discussed them so often with my friends. Dear darling Sebastian, it is getting to beat any moment that ever was in the whole world when I close some door behind me, and find you there as dear as ever and smiling and happy and sane. We have only been given a few minutes altogether to write this letter and turn it in for dispatch, and probably when I have sent it off I will remember a dozen things I should have told you about. But you will understand ...

See you soon. Believe and remember Sunny, I love you with all my heart. Alan'

A day later he wrote again. He still had some medical duties to perform, but otherwise he was preoccupied in imagining their meeting.

'This is a sudden unexpected chance to send you a letter which may get home sooner than our first official ones which were written yesterday. I have just been told to select some patients from my wards for immediate evacuation by air, and one of them will take this for me. Being, as usual, always working (!) there was no chance of putting my own name at the head of the list. Poor Sebastian!

This will sound awful nonsense if it does happen to be the first news you get from me, but things here are absolutely chaotic. So they have been for the last couple of weeks and I hardly know whether I am on my head or my heels. However, I am still the same as ever as far as my own judgement can guide me, and my only important loss has been of three of my teeth. Luckily none of the gaps show, so you should be able to recognize me all right. You will find me, for one thing, loving you in exactly the same way as always. There hasn't been a single day when I haven't done my best to get as close to you as possible, and as far as I am concerned being free means only being free to be with you again.

I have no intention of trying to tell you anything about the past three and a half years now. That will all trickle out in due course, but at the moment I am very well, but poisonously overworked ... There is plenty of excitement, but I am so tied down to my patients and rounds that I can't nip out and take my fair share of it. Most of the chaps are doing nothing at all now, so you can imagine what a colossal amount of gossiping and smoking and tea drinking they are going in for. Also listening to news broadcasts from wireless loud-speakers set up all over the camp.

So far there has been nothing to drink (in the important sense) but I expect someone will produce a bottle of beer any day now. This morning I had some fun when two girls appeared in my domain. They were very nice girls and fairly made the patients sit up. When someone made a joke and the girls laughed it was an astounding sound – really the best thing I have heard for years.'

Believing that his second letter would reach her before his first, he repeated his earlier request that she meet him at the Cumberland Hotel:

'It may be hard for you to know when to book, but there has been such a flap in the papers about the poor prisoners of war that I am

sure they would make special concessions for you if you put the case fairly to them. As soon as possible I shall cable telling you when I may be expected. I badly want you to be in London before me, so that I can take a taxi or a rickshaw or whatever they have and shout "to the Cumberland", and be off at a hard gallop. This is the way I have always visualized it, although I must say my imagination has never been able to take me beyond the moment when I close the door of your room behind me, and find you there as real as you ever were. I hope it will be all right. Anyway I have written a most beautiful sonnet, which I'll show you one of these days, about our meeting. I haven't made it in any hotel (not poetic!) but I have said that once we are together again, none of this will be important at all . . .

Darling, as well as being happy I am worried too. I have had many of your letters . . . but my latest news is from last November – nearly a year ago. I am hoping with all my heart that everything is still as good now as it was then.

. . . I am just about passing out at the thought of seeing you – still quite faithful, and loving you with all my heart.'

On 15 September, Alan was one of 2,000 to embark on the 15,000-ton Dutch transport *Tegelberg* for repatriation to Europe. Four days into his voyage he wrote to Joy again.

'Since my other letter I have nothing fresh to report except the breeze on the boat deck which has been delicious. I am loving the sea too, and thinking of it connecting me with you all round the world without a break. It was one of the oddnesses of being in the bag that when I did get a glimpse of the sea it didn't help at all. In

fact it was one of the few things which ever made me miserable. There it was – the broad road to freedom – and not the least smallest chance of travelling it. And now I am well on the way. You can guess at the difference. My bunk is an upper one just beneath an open scuttle, and I can see the blue waves rushing and tumbling past. I love them.'

The *Tegelberg* docked at Liverpool early on the morning of 15 October. A railway strike was in progress but a volunteer was found to take a train to London.

The longed-for rendezvous at the Cumberland was on.

Postscript

This sonnet was composed by Alan Glendinning as a prisoner of war on the back of the only piece of paper to hand, an acknowledgement written twenty years before of a letter from the Malayan inspector of prisons reporting on Raub Prison. For the soldier longing to return to loved ones at home, its sentiments are universal.

December 1943

One day I'll rest my elbows on the rail
Of some proud ship, and feel her softly glide,
Immense above the oily urban side,
Into a dock, where hail on answering hail
Will mark again this old romantic tale,
A ship safe home. And as I stand aside
To scan the faces upturned on the wide
Bright quay, you will not, in your dearness, fail
To come to me unchanged across the years.
And when I take your brown remembered hands,
A moment hold you close against my heart,
The sudden bitter happiness of tears
Wished too long in far unfriendly lands
Will tell me we have never been apart.